YES INDEED!

It Takes a Village!

A Model for Education

LILA BURDETT

Annandale Press
Vancouver, BC, Canada

Copyright © 2012 by Lila Burdett
www.lilaburdett.com
lilaburdett@hotmail.com

Available from Amazon.com.

ISBN: 978-1-77136-065-4 (paperback)

Maps by Lila Burdett
Cover designed by Tiffanee J.A. Griffiths

CONTENTS

This book is dedicated to
The Upper Similkameen Indian Band
and the
Lower Similkameen Indian Band

ACKNOWLEDGEMENTS

I wish to thank the people of the Similkameen Native community and the Keremeos school district staff who gave freely of their time and thoughts for this study. They have accomplished remarkable success in the field of Native Indian education. My study revealed that the guiding lights in this endeavor for almost four decades because of their vision were Barney Allison and Bobby Allison.

I am grateful to Dr. David Williams and Dr. Clark Webb for their time and guidance.

My thanks to Joann Vriend for sharing information on First Nations education in Dawson City, Yukon.

I wish to thank two people who stepped forward to encourage me to make this study accessible to others: Dr. Louise Jilek-Aall, and William Butler, for his editorial skills, support and assistance throughout this endeavor. Special thanks also to my nephews Sean Butler and Patrick Butler for their help in navigating the publishing process. Sean Butler also took responsibility for formatting the book.

My special appreciation, gratitude and love to my husband John Butler, who stood by me each step of the way. My love to my family Shannon Kilroy, Joseph Pierre, Shawn Kilroy, Tiffanee Griffiths, Laine Pare, Ian Pierre, Phoenix Moosewaypayo and Reiken Moosewaypayo.

INTRODUCTION

Over 93% of students from the Similkameen Indian Band in British Columbia Canada graduate from high school. This success began in 1963 and continues to the present - a period of 50 years. The original research for this study was done in 1991 and was updated in 2012.

In 2012 Marcus Toneatto, principal of the Similkameen Elementary Secondary School in the town of Keremeos, stated "Graduation rates of students from the Similkameen Band are very high. The Similkameen Band is very supportive of education." He further commented on the positive attitude of the teaching staff toward Native students and added, "There are more Native students on sports teams and taking leadership classes than in any other district I have worked in." Jim Insley, assistant superintendent of the school district which includes the town of Keremeos said, "The students of the

Similkameen Band have strong graduation rates. They are supported by strong, educated parents and it makes a difference."

I grew up in the town of Keremeos. When I was in school the academic success of Native students wasn't commented on, it was taken for granted that they would graduate with their classmates. It wasn't until I became a teacher and taught Native students in several districts throughout British Columbia, that I realized what a unique situation existed in the Similkameen Valley. When I returned to university to study for a Doctorate in Education I decided to investigate the reasons for this success as part of my research. Could the reasons for the exceptional success of the Native students in the valley be identified ? If so, would they be transferable to other school districts to help other students?

I decided to conduct a naturalistic study based on interviews, observations and a review of relevant literature. I returned to the Similkameen Valley to interview members of the Similkameen Indian Band and teachers and administrators at local schools.

I identified several factors that contributed to the high graduation rate of Native students in the Similkameen Valley. Many of these factors could be encouraged by other communities to increase the graduation rates of their students. The factors are: a positive history regarding white people; minimal attendance of parents at residential schools; integration of Native and white population; encouragement of students by parents and family members; support for students from the Similkameen Band; support for students from school staff; strong role models for students; involvement of the majority of students in school sports. Each of these factors has contributed to the educational success of the students.

CHAPTER 1

EDUCATIONAL SUCCESS IN THE SIMILKAMEEN VALLEY

"Sports hold kids. Changes their whole view of school. Indian kids in the Similkameen are good athletes."   Jeanine Terbasket

To tell this story, which is based on research I conducted in 1991 and have since updated, I included interviews with members of the Similkameen Indian Band and interviews with teachers and staff of the Keremeos school district. I included a description of the Similkameen Indian reserve lands, information about myself and my connection with the people of the Similkameen Indian Band. I also included information bearing on the attitudes and beliefs that have shaped the Similkameen Band and influenced their outlook on education. These attitudes and beliefs are basic to the exceptionally high graduation rate of students from the Band. I have quoted Band members quite extensively, wishing to use their own words. Only one person spoke too quickly to record everything relevant. In this case I was able to record important information and summarize the rest of the interview. The names of the people from the Similkameen Indian community that were interviewed are listed in the order in which they were introduced. I hope that the information included will enable people to make comparisons with situations within their own communities.

Similkameen Indian Reserves

(Based on *Community Profile of the Similkameen Native Community: 1985* by D. Nairne.)

The Similkameen Indian Bands have sixteen reserves covering approximately 44,000 acres distributed throughout the Similkameen River Valley, located in the south central region of British Columbia (see Appendix A). The seven reserves belonging to the Upper Similkameen Band make up fifteen percent of the land base. In this area adjacent to the small village of Hedley, a retirement community with a population of approximately 425, narrow flatland meadows and hayfields are surrounded by steep walled mountains cut by numerous shale slides. Further south the eighty-five percent of the land belonging to the Lower Similkameen Band is in a broader, flatter part of the valley. Approximately twenty-five percent of the land is owned by individual Band members. The remainder is owned by the Band (Nairne, 1985, p.13). Twenty percent of all the land is suitable for agriculture. The remainder is used for forestry, range and hunting.

The climate in this region is semi-arid and during the summer "predominantly westerly winds make Keremeos one of the hottest, driest areas in Canada" (Nairne, p. 21). The total population for the Lower Similkameen Valley from Hedley to the American border, a distance of 30 miles, is 3500. Keremeos has a population of 830. The nearest village to the Lower Similkameen Reserves is Cawston with a population of approximately 380.

"The settlement pattern within the Similkameen Bands' reserves has a typically rural character. The houses are spread out, usually on large parcels of land near or adjacent to transportation routes" (Nairne, p. 80). The most northerly reserve is Chuchuwayha near Hedley. It is the site of a small picturesque Catholic church that sits on a hill overlooking the surrounding area and eight homes. Eight miles further south on the Ashnola Reserve there is a new subdivision with several homes. A short distance further up the road is the Pow-wow Grounds. It contains a circular pow-wow pavilion built of logs that has twelve sections of roofed bleachers. The grounds also contain a log cook house, shower rooms, concessions and a large open camping area. The Pow-wow Grounds are situated between high rocky mountains and Ashnola Creek.

Blind Creek Reserve near Cawston is ten miles south of Ashnola. It contains several homes, the Tee Pee Tot Day Care Centre, and the Similkameen

Indian Administration Field Office. Twelve miles further south on the Skemeoskuankin Reserve on the American border, also known as the Chopaka Reserve, there are numerous homes, a Catholic church, rodeo grounds and picnic grounds.

The Similkameen people have developed an economy based on traditional activities (hunting, fishing, gathering berries and other natural foods) as well as on occupations brought by the Europeans (ranching, farming and logging). Due to the seasonal nature of much of the work, forty-four percent of the labor force receives social assistance for part of the year.

Both Similkameen Bands are governed by their own elected Chief and Councillors. These elected officials are the legislative assembly for the Native community. Their decisions are carried out by the Similkameen Indian Administration (SIA), which is the executive and administrative arm of the Councils. The chief executive officer for the Bands is the Band Administrator. "Since 1969 when the Bands first began to take on administrative functions, the organization has grown to...a full-time staff of twelve, as well as several part-time workers" (Nairne, p.26).

The population of the Similkameen Band is approximately 250. Eighty-five percent of the people belong to the Lower Similkameen Band. The population is gradually increasing. It is projected that eventually seventy-five percent of Band members will live on-reserve, up from the present seventy percent. The Band has a young population, a large number of them are 24 years of age or younger. As the population ages the Band will face increased pressures for employment and accommodation.

Major areas of social concern for members of the Similkameen community are alcohol and drug abuse. They "...are of particular concern, given their close relationship to other problems such as accidents, violence and deaths. The Bands have their own drug and alcohol counsellor" (Nairne, p. 39).

At the local elementary and high schools Native students make up about twelve percent of the population, approximately seventy-five students out of 600 students in the district. The schools are situated three to twelve miles from the reserves. Cawston and Hedley each have a primary school with kindergarten through grade three. The Similkameen Elementary Secondary School, with a population of 440 students, is centrally located at Keremeos. It is a modern building laid out in two wings. The elementary wing is a recent addition and houses two classes each of grades four through seven, and contains its own gym. It replaced the original elementary school which was torn down about 1985. The renovated secondary wing contains grades eight through twelve. It is a well equipped school with a modern library, three computer labs, a two storey music room with individual practice rooms and two Special Education classrooms.

My Story

I was born in Pioneer Mine, a small gold mining town situated in the mountains of coastal British Columbia that has since become a ghost town. When I was one month old my family moved to Quesnel, a midsize town in the north central region of the province and then to Keremeos in the Similkameen Valley when I was five. We resided in Keremeos for sixteen years on a small fruit farm where we raised a few head of cattle. My father drove bulldozer for the Department of Highways. I was the second child and first daughter in a family of four.

At the age of sixteen, after completing grade ten, I married Joe Kilroy, a twenty year old Native logger. He was living with relatives on the Upper Similkameen Reserve fifteen miles north of Keremeos. He was a member of the Thompson Indian Band at Merritt, a community one hundred miles to the north. I went to live with him in a small cabin near his family on the Upper Similkameen Reserve. I attributed our subsequent marriage problems to his dependence on alcohol rather than to cultural differences. Having grown up in Keremeos where many of the Native people were well-to-do ranchers and all residents of the valley were accepted as equals, I was unaware that there were any cultural differences between Native and white people.

The birth of our daughter Shannon a year after the marriage marked the beginning of a five year separation. I moved home to live with my family and when my daughter was a year old, I enrolled at the Similkameen Secondary School to continue my education. After I graduated I spent two years at the University of Victoria studying to be a teacher. During this time my family moved to Merritt, a ranching and mining town which had a population of 8000.

Completion of my second year at university earned me a teaching certificate. My first teaching assignment was a class of forty-two grade three and four students in a small school five miles north of Merritt at Lower Nicola. The school was located a mile from the Shulus Indian Reserve where my husband lived. It was 1964 and Native Indian students had only recently been allowed to leave residential schools and attend local public schools. Approximately one-third of the students at Lower Nicola School were from the reserves at Shulus and Canford. I was appalled at the way Native students were singled out whenever a group was needed for an educational experiment. The school principal's philosophy was, "Use the Indian kids. Their parents won't make a fuss."

At Christmas that year my husband and I reconciled. With our five year old daughter, we moved into a small house on the Shulus Reserve. My principal was dismayed that one of his teachers would live on an Indian reserve, and I sometimes noticed that colleagues who were friendly to me at school would cross the street if they saw me in town with my husband. On the reserve most people made me feel welcome but some chose to ignore me. The cultural problems I had never recognized were becoming more obvious. The two years I spent teaching at

Lower Nicola marked the beginning of my interest in the education of Native Indian students.

After two and a half years my husband and I again separated. I took my daughter to Saskatchewan where I taught a grade two-three class for a year in the small town of Turtleford. I had the opportunity to work with Cree Indian children who came to school fluent in the Cree language but speaking no English. I observed that these children were bright and curious with a strong sense of self-worth similar to the Similkameen Indian children.

After spending the following summer at the University of Victoria, I moved to Port Alberni, a pulp and paper center in the middle of Vancouver Island. The grade three to five class I taught included a small number of Native children from coastal and northern reserves. They lived at the residential school while attending classes in the public schools. Many of them came from isolated villages and were sent to live in residential school because of poverty and family breakdown.

At the end of my first year in Port Alberni my daughter and I returned to the Upper Similkameen Reserve for the summer to reconcile for a second time with my husband. We moved fifty miles southeast to Oroville, a small town in Washington state, where Joe worked for the summer on a ranch. In the fall we returned to Port Alberni where I continued teaching school and Joe went to work in the forest industry.

At the end of the school year we moved to the Upper Similkameen Reserve to await the birth of our second child, a son. When Shawn was four months old, I began to fulfill a request my sister-in-law, Carrie Allison, had made of me years before. "Someday when you have time, I want you to teach me." Carrie had a grade three education from the Indian residential school at Kamloops but had always dreamed of getting more schooling. She had decided that this was the time. Because several of the adults on the Upper and Lower Similkameen reserves expressed an interest in going to school, *If you're going to teach Carrie, I want you to teach me,*" I contacted the Department of Indian Affairs in

Vancouver. They agreed to fund the class, supplying all books and materials. Two evenings a week for five months I made the twenty-five mile trip to the Chopaka reserve to teach the class. Twenty people, including the chiefs of both Bands, met at the hall on the lower reserve to go to school. I taught grades one through ten, encouraging people to start at their comfort level and progress at their own speed.

Although I left the district before the following winter Carrie and the other Band members found another teacher. They kept the night school going for three more winters, until they had completed the level of education they needed to achieve their ambitions. Carrie then studied for a year to become a hairdresser and two of the other women, Theresa Ann Terbasket and Hazel Squakin, trained as Native Court Workers. The latter two have since qualified as linguists in the Okanagan language and Hazel went to university to become a teacher.

After spending the next summer at the University of Victoria, and feeling the need to return to fulltime work, I moved with my family to a teaching position for the Department of Indian Affairs (DIA) in the isolated Native coastal village of Kingcome Inlet, 200 miles north of Vancouver. The village was accessible only by boat or floatplane. I had been warned that there were no stores, and that the post office was located in a farmer's house a five mile boat trip down river from the village. We flew in and took our first month's supply of groceries with us. After that I had to order each month's supply of groceries in advance from the Woodwards store in Vancouver. The groceries were brought by barge and unloaded on a large float surrounded by water seven miles down the river. We would arrange for one of the men from the village to pick up the supplies in a large motorized canoe. Everything was then unloaded on the beach and Joe would bring the boxes up to the house. I taught a grade four through seven class which included my daughter Shannon, who was in grade seven. The only other teacher in the village was the chief's wife, who taught grades one to three in a newer one room structure beside the small building where I taught.

Working for a local logging company, Joe had several hair raising experiences. After rowing across the wide, often dangerous, Kingcome River before dawn each day and walking a mile through thick, dark forest to the main logging road, he would be picked up by crew members who lived in the logging camp two miles north of Kingcome Village. Often, when returning home in the evening, he would find fresh wolf tracks and grizzly bear droppings on the trail. Joe made this daily trek alone because, although other men in the village were loggers, none of them worked for that logging company.

One day in October it became obvious that, due to heavy rains, the river would reach flood proportions by evening. Other loggers from the village, familiar with the dangers of the rainy season, had stayed home that day but Joe had gone to work as usual. When he returned to the far edge of the river, I was standing with several of the villagers on the shore watching helplessly as he, an inexperienced boatman, attempted to maneuver across the raging, swirling waters. His greatest challenge was avoiding dozens of fallen trees hurtling down the river. A cheer of relief went up as the men helped him pull the boat up on shore.

The river rose over its banks, flooding the village for several days. Except for the loggers, no one was particularly inconvenienced. Because of frequent flooding, houses were built on stilts and each family kept a boat tied near their door. Since the single path through the two mile stretch of village was underwater, people rowed wherever they went. Even the students rowed to school. So adept were the older children that they could center themselves in the middle of a small boat, standing on one foot and rowing with the other, dipping their foot in the water and pulling as if it were an oar.

As rain continued to pour day after day, numerous newly created waterfalls thundered down the steep sides of the mountains surrounding the village. The beauty and music of those falls is etched forever in my memory.

Although I had only fourteen students to teach, aged nine to fourteen years old, it was a challenging experience. Since the village was isolated, the children seldom had opportunity to visit other areas. One of their entertainments and yearly challenges was to rid themselves of the new teacher as early in the school year as possible. The chief's young adult son would then become their teacher for the remainder of the school year.

It was a deep snow winter and all logging operations came to a standstill by Christmas. At the end of February, Joe said he had had enough of the enforced idleness. It was with mixed feelings of regret and relief that I resigned my teaching post. In spite of the stresses of isolation, we had established close friendships among the villagers.

Returning to Merritt, we purchased a mobile home and moved it onto land we owned on the Shulus Reserve. Joe went to work at the local copper mine. In August I accepted a position as Native Indian Home-School Coordinator with the Merritt School District. That fall Joe and I separated for the last time, divorcing a year later.

As Home-School Coordinator my job was to work between local schools and homes on six reserves, helping to find solutions to educational problems. The experience made me aware of progress that had been made in Native education during my absence from Merritt and of how much work was still to be done. The following year I returned to the classroom, teaching an alternate class of predominantly Native students aged ten to fifteen years.

Leaving Merritt after three years, I returned with my children to Port Alberni for a three year period. During that time I taught a combined grade two-three class and became involved in local Native education projects. When my daughter graduated from high school and entered college in Nanaimo, I moved with my son Shawn, then seven years old, to Vancouver where I enrolled at the University of British Columbia. I completed the fifth year of a Bachelor of Education and a Masters Degree in Educational Administration.

Soon after that I accepted a teaching position with the Department of Indian Affairs on the Kitwancool Indian Reserve. With my present husband, John Butler, and my son, I took a twenty hour ferry trip north from Vancouver to Prince Rupert, then drove two hours east to Kitwancool. On the reserve there was an elementary school with four teachers. I was to teach twenty students in the primary grades. High school students were bussed twelve miles to the public high school in Kitwanga which had both Native and white students.

Kitwancool Reserve is known for having refused to allow either church leaders or the police force to coerce them into sending their children to residential school at anytime during the 1920s through the 1950s. We were told that the men from the reserve met the authorities with guns on the road to the reserve and made clear their feelings with regard to sending their children to residential school. For this reason there were few wounds to heal regarding education and parents were supportive of the local schools.

The following year my family and I moved to Quesnel, a town of 10,000 people, four hundred miles north of Vancouver. In the Quesnel school district I taught an alternate class for Native Indian children who needed help catching up to their grade level. There were twelve children aged seven to sixteen in grades one through seven. It was a rewarding experience because several of the children reached their grade level. They were able to return to a regular class the following year. When the class was disbanded after two years I accepted a grade four position in the district.

A year and a half later the Vancouver School District employed me to develop a pilot program for Native Indian students in grades four through seven. The purpose of the program was to increase the retention rate of Native students in high school and thereby to increase the number of Native graduates.

While doing this I became involved in the development of an educational resource guide for Native education. It was based on a set of paintings of successful contemporary Native Indian people that were published in a book titled <u>Chronicles of Pride</u>. The paintings were done by artist Patricia Richardson Logie. The book detailed the accomplishments of each of the people portrayed. The resource guide outlined lesson plans and suggestions for teachers to use in presenting the subjects of the paintings to their classes as inspirations and role models. As the project progressed I realized that I enjoyed curriculum development. It inspired me to apply to Brigham Young University in Utah and I was accepted into the Doctor of Education program majoring in Curriculum and Instruction.

The years I had worked in Native education had made me aware of the problems being experienced by Native Indian students and by educators working with them. I had become aware of the lack of success in Native education and that it was a widespread problem throughout Canada and the United States.

Because the unique situation regarding the high graduation rate of Native Indian students in the Similkameen Valley puzzled me, I decided to investigate it for my dissertation. I wanted to try to discover if any of the components involved would be transferable to other school districts to help improve the educational opportunities of other Native Indian students.

Members of the Similkameen Native Indian Community Who Were Interviewed

Edward (Slim) Allison - Chief of Upper Similkameen Band

Carrie Allison - hairdresser

Nora Allison - attended residential school

Jeanine Terbasket - Similkameen graduate

Janet Terbasket - Similkameen graduate

Wendy Terbasket - Similkameen graduate

Karen Terbasket - Similkameen graduate

John Terbasket - traditional elder

Philip - non-Native employee of the Band

Frank Qualtier - Similkameen graduate

Barnett (Barney) Allison - Chief of Lower Similkameen Band

Nancy (Nan) Allison - Manager of "The Basketball Club"

Carol Allison - Similkameen graduate

Theresa Ann Terbasket - Community Health Representative

Debbie Crow - Home School Coordinator for school district

Albert Heinrich - Similkameen graduate

Marcy Trotter - Native Counsellor/Tutor for school district

Theresa Sam - originally from Fort St. John, B. C.

Leon Louis - graduate; traditional Indian medicine and religion

Barbara Allison - Similkameen graduate

Henry Allison - bus driver for school district

Twenty-two members of the Similkameen Indian community were approached and asked to take part in this study. These included high school graduates, members of their families, and other members of the Upper and Lower Similkameen Bands. Sixteen educators in the Keremeos school district were also included. People interviewed often suggested other individuals that would be valuable for me to interview. There are many more people that could be included but for the story I am telling in this book, I will focus on these participants. The interview of each informant is written in a storytelling format with specific quotations taken from interview notes. Although some people were interviewed several times, each is portrayed in a single composite interview.

My relationship with the Similkameen Valley and with the Native people of the area provides a thread throughout the story. I have included three Native people that are long-term residents of the valley but who grew up in other communities. They have a unique perspective to offer on factors influencing education in the area. Also interviewed were six people who attended Native Indian residential schools.

When I went to the Similkameen to do research for my study I stayed with my in-laws, Carrie and Slim Allison, on the Upper Similkameen Reserve situated three miles south of Hedley on the TransCanada Highway. They live in a three bedroom ranchstyle house to which is attached Carrie's beauty salon. It is in a portable unit across a paved covered breezeway from the house.

I arrived on a rainy day in April to begin my first week of interviews. After supper that evening, I asked Carrie and Slim to tell me about their experiences while attending Indian residential schools.

Chief Edward (Slim) Allison

Edward (Slim) Allison, chief of the Upper Nicola Band, grew up on the ranch where he and Carrie live. Through the north kitchen window Carrie showed me the location of the original family home. A couple of posts are all that is left of the burned building. The smaller house that Slim's family lived in after that has since been moved to the back of the property.

Slim told me stories of his schooling:

"I was six or seven when I first went to school in Hedley. I was too small to walk the three miles from home. The first year I lived with Johnny Holmes' mother and the second I lived with Dan Toma's mother. By grade three I was old enough to walk to school. I went through grade six in Hedley. The Indians donated land at Hedley for a school so that the Indian kids could go to school there.

"In 1939, when I was thirteen years old, I went to Cranbrook Residential School (in the

Kootenay area about two hundred forty miles east of Hedley). I wouldn't go back again after that year. We only went to school three hours a day. We worked the other half day. We didn't do enough work to complete a full year of schooling. It took me all the next year at Hedley to finish grade seven. The year after that I did grade eight. When I passed into grade nine I quit school. I think they would have let me go on higher if I had wanted to. At Keremeos (a long time ago) Indian kids were only allowed to go to grade four. On the Lower Similkameen Reserve, most kids went to Cranbrook Residential School because they lived too far from school. The kids at Upper Similkameen went to school at Hedley or to the residential school at Cranbrook.

"In the Similkameen Valley everyone was treated the same (Indians and whites) at school and on the job. Indians who came from other areas were surprised by this. I never felt any prejudice either at school or on the job."

Carrie Allison

Carrie was born into the Thompson Indian nation on the Shulus Reserve at Merritt, British Columbia, eighty miles north of Hedley. She was a member of the Lower Nicola Band. At six years of age she began to attend the day school at Shulus.

"I only went there for two years, then the priests started making us go to the residential school. I think I would have done better at school if they'd left me at Shulus because we were a close family. The school went up to grade eight. They came around in the fall with cattle trucks. They'd round up all the kids, whether they wanted to go or not, and take them to the residential school. When they made us go to Kamloops, we were away from our family. We were lonely, we didn't have enough to eat, and they were so strict. We never got to go home till the next summer. It was sixty miles and we had no way to get there.

"When the nuns asked, `*Who can sew?*' I said, `*I can,*' because my mother had taught me. After that, they had me doing mending for the whole time I was at the school. I even mended socks. And I was only eight years old. Can you imagine making an eight year old do something like that?" Carrie shook her head.

"We had to keep the whole school clean. Everyday we'd go to school half a day and work half a day. The kids were always hungry. Even though the school had a farm and raised all their own food. The vegetables were the only thing the kids got. I think they used to boil bones in the water, then put the vegetables in. Slim still won't eat vegetables. The school raised cattle and canned their own fruit. The staff ate really well. We used to have to serve them and we'd see that they got plates piled high with meat and potatoes. They had cakes and cookies for dessert. It always seemed like the nuns counted things like cookies, so if we got a craving for sugar we'd sneak some from the sugar bowl so they wouldn't miss it."

Slim and Carrie's recollections added to other disturbing stories I had heard about residential schools.

Nora Allison

While we were talking, Slim's niece, Nora, arrived. She shared with me some of her experiences during her brief stay at the Cranbrook Residential School during the early 1950s. Nora went to the school when she was fourteen years old. She realized after three or four weeks that she didn't want to stay. She said the school was nice but she didn't like one of the nuns. When she told the head sister that she wanted to go home, she was told she couldn't go until June. Nora sneaked upstairs to see the priest who was the principal. He wrote to her dad. Charlie said to send her on the train and he would send the money. After that she did the rest of her schooling in Hedley.

Nora also gave me her views on education in the Similkameen Valley. She felt her three kids had been as well accepted in school as the white kids. "Many whites think more of the Indians than they do of the other whites. Most of the rodeo queens here for years have been Indian." Nora pointed out five recent examples.

She also feels that money talks. "If the people were dirt poor, they probably wouldn't be as well treated." She thinks that some form of traditional religion or belief system has always been kept by most of the families in the valley. Nora's parents, Charlie and Mary Allison, were strong Catholics. "They didn't drink. They were in church all the time. They took care of the church and the priest and cared about everybody."

The morning after I arrived, I was to begin interviewing members of the Similkameen Bands at the Similkameen Indian Administration Office in Keremeos. The administration office functions similarly to a Town Office. As Carrie and I drove the ten miles into town, I told her I was nervous because there were so many of the younger people I didn't know. They had grown up since I'd been gone.

Her reaction was, "You shouldn't be nervous. I'll introduce them to you." Carrie never seems nervous around anyone.

Entering the town limits, we drove past several fruit orchards that were coming into leaf and passed several fruitstands closed for the season. I parked in front of the band office, wondering why there was a gold covered couch sitting on the sidewalk in front of the building. No one ever explained why it was there and I forgot to ask.

Inside the office, which is a converted movie theatre, there were three hardbacked chairs against the wall on the right-hand side of the waiting room. On the left-hand side were two similar chairs and a coffee table covered with some pamphlets. Straight ahead was the office area where a circular counter opened into the waiting room.

Several months earlier when I had described my project to Carrie in a telephone conversation, she had suggested I interview John Terbasket's family because all six of the girls had graduated from grade twelve. When we arrived that day all the girls, Karen, Lauren, Wendy, Jeanine, Janet and Kathy were behind the counter in the office. Although Lauren was attending Nicola Valley Institute of Technology in

Merritt, a postsecondary institution for Native people, she was home for Easter weekend. I had phoned ahead, so they were expecting me.

When Carrie introduced us, Karen, the eldest, said she was busy right then but asked her sisters if some of them could talk to me. They were very friendly and the three youngest ones, Jeanine, Janet and Wendy said they'd be glad to. They wanted to know how long I would need because they were getting ready to go to a pow-wow (a traditional spiritual Native Indian ceremony involving dancing and singing) in Coeur d' Alene, Idaho.

As Jeanine and Janet ushered me into the first office down the right-hand hall of the building, they explained that for years their family has participated regularly in pow-wows all over western Canada and the United States. Their parents had started taking the girls when they were younger and had encouraged them to become involved in the dancing. Their intention was to keep them busy on holidays and to keep them away from drugs and alcohol. Drugs and alcohol aren't allowed at pow-wows. "There's nothing in Keremeos except sports and the bar. Take your choice," was the way Jeanine summed it up.

Janet told me that Wendy would join us in a few minutes so we started without her. The six sisters ranged in age from nineteen to twenty-nine. I remarked to myself how different they were in appearance. I wouldn't have been able to pick them out as sisters in a crowd. Jeanine, Janet, Wendy, Kathy and Lauren were all involved in athletics and had the slim figures associated with sports. They all had long hair.

The girls explained that they come from a politically oriented family and have always travelled a lot. Both parents strongly pushed them to go to school. Their mother, Delphine, graduated from high school and took one or two years of nurse's training.

They explained that their family had been very influenced by John's uncles, Barney Allison, chief of the Lower Similkameen Band, and his older brother Bobby, both prosperous ranchers. They had wanted to be successful like them. John, whose parents had died when he was quite young, had been raised by his Uncle Barney and Auntie Margaret, after spending several years in residential school in Cranbrook. John and Delphine already had three daughters when Barney and Bobby convinced John to take courses at the Cody Institute in Antigonish, Nova Scotia. Barney and Bobby had spent some time with Indian leaders from other areas, including Andy Paul of the Squamish Nation, near Vancouver. This had made them aware of some of the future needs of the Band. They wanted John to study a community planning course in alcoholism, community instability, etc. He was then to come back and help his community. This was in 1966. John was working in an orchard in Palmer Lake, Washington when Barney and Bobby approached him. They gave him two weeks to make up his mind. John agreed to go if he could take his family with him. Jeanine was born during the year in Nova Scotia.

When the band office was first set up in Keremeos in 1969 John became the administrator and his wife was the accountant. At that time over ninety per cent of the people in the Band had drinking problems. John and Delphine had been among the first to stop drinking. The younger girls don't remember ever seeing their dad drink. The older girls do. They described their parents as changing from alcoholics to workaholics. In a separate interview with Karen, she explained that she and Lauren, the two oldest daughters, felt that they were left to look after the home and raise their younger sisters during this period. Their parents got very involved working in the Band office right from the very beginning.

Jeanine: "Dad feels his family suffered because of his commitment to the community. He was so busy that we hardly saw him when he was Band administrator. He worked from 7:00 A.M. until 6:00 P.M. at the Band office." The girls agree that their father laid a strong foundation for the Similkameen Band.

Several years ago their parents divorced and their mother has since married a Native American from Yakima, Washington. It was obvious the girls were still adjusting to this change in their lives.

Jeanine Terbasket

During the interview Jeanine, the fourth daughter, played with her hair, putting it into a ponytail, loosening the elastic band until the hair fell loose on her shoulders, then putting it back into a ponytail. She was dressed in knee-length black stretch shorts with a pink side stripe and a white shirt open at the neck. She explained to me that at pow-wows she used to do traditional dancing but stopped seven or eight years ago when she got too busy because of her studies.

After graduating from school in Keremeos, Jeanine completed a double major in Political Science and Indian Studies at the University of Regina/Saskatchewan Indian Federated College in Saskatchewan. She then entered a three year law program at the University of British Columbia.

When I asked the girls whether they had ever experienced prejudice in the Similkameen Valley, Jeanine was very candid in her remarks. "I first noticed prejudice when I went to school in Regina. There's a lot of prejudice there. The kids in this valley are not taught to look for prejudice. Therefore they often don't recognize it and overlook it when it does occur. I see that as being very positive. I didn't have the trouble my friends had with prejudice in Regina. I wasn't submissive. I didn't expect trouble. I think it was to do with attitude. Being raised in Keremeos makes a difference. Maybe the first generations got along well with the white people and it's carried on. It's built into this community, carried down through the generations. Most Indians, women and men, bring their mates back to Keremeos because it's such a great place to live." (It's traditional in other areas for men to take their wives back to the husband's reserve.)

Regarding education in Keremeos Jeanine commented, "Similkameen Secondary School is a small school so it's harder to fall through the cracks. You know everyone. The teachers are supportive and they give you a break. Some teachers have taught two or three generations of kids. One problem was Special Education. In our age group most kids who weren't `jocks' were pushed into Special Ed and couldn't get out. The parents started getting really scared of

Special Ed because it was a dead end. Kids came out with very few skills. The school is making a special effort now to mainstream Special Ed kids, partly because of pressure from the (Similkameen) Band. Parents in the Similkameen Valley say to their kids, `Go to school and get a good job or be stuck on the ranch forever.'

"Sports hold kids. Changes their whole view of school. Indian kids in the Similkameen are good athletes. They do well in basketball, volleyball, baseball, track-and-field. They're on all the teams. Even in grades five, six and seven, kids are really into sports - soccer, basketball, baseball."

Janet Terbasket

Janet, the fifth daughter, was dressed in jeans and a waist length jacket. Her curly hair was shoulder length. She was quieter than Jeanine and took longer to warm up to sharing with me. Once she got started she shared quite openly.

When Janet was younger she told her parents she only wanted to go to grade ten, but changed her mind because of sports once she was in high school. Janet likes the outdoors. Forestry and policing are her career interests. Two years earlier she enrolled in the Nicola Valley Institute of Technology (NVIT) in Merritt to take upgrading to complete grade twelve and to study forestry. She was scared when she went there but got into sports again and felt more comfortable. Then she entered a peace-keeping (Native policing) course. She was part of the second group to be trained in British Columbia. She hoped to eventually work in the Similkameen Valley.

Janet explained to me that at pow-wows she jingle dances. Toward the end of the interview she went out to the car and brought in a zippered suitbag. Out of it she took her jingle dress and leggings. It looked like a European folkstyle dress. All over the front of the dress were attached tiny bells hammered out of the lids of beer cans. She explained that the bells jingled when she danced. Obviously many hours of work had gone into preparing the beautiful costume. Janet told me she had really liked jingle dancing when she watched it at pow-wows, so she decided to become a jingle dancer herself.

Janet and Jeanine agreed, "We've always been John and Delphine's daughters. That's had a big effect on us. People expected us to keep going to school and to do well for that reason."

Jeanine: "My mom really pushed me to go to school. She really wanted me to do law. Dad wanted me to go to school but to do what I wanted.

"Lauren (the second eldest daughter) had straight A's. She's really smart like Mom. She dropped out of school at sixteen or seventeen. Mom was really disappointed because she had wanted Lauren to become a lawyer. Later she went back and finished school. Then she went to NVIT in Merritt to study Economic Development."

It was taken for granted the girls would go on to school. The question was not "if" but "what" they would study next and "where".

They told me that Kathy the third sister went to Regina to upgrade through grade twelve. She now works at the band office as a secretary and is taking courses in band management. Although I tried several times to involve Kathy in my project, she declined to take part. Her sisters described her as "headstrong," and said she didn't "fall in line" like the others.

Jeanine said, regarding relationships between Native and white people in the valley: "There are rednecks on both sides. There are a few Indian people here who can't stand white people. At school, older Indian kids looked out for younger ones (in an inconspicuous way). This was an unspoken code. You look out for your friends. If there were redneck types, their behavior was quickly squashed by older Indian kids.

"There was no difference between white and Indian kids. We had lots of Indian friends and white friends at school. We dated white boys and had them for friends but never seriously considered them as marriage partners. There's an understanding in our family (a look, an attitude) that we won't marry a white person. It's never really stated by our parents but there's a feeling that the two cultures don't mesh well." Jeanine cited some local examples. There is also a concern that once a white person starts living on the reserve, some of the land may eventually be lost to the reserve. This has happened in the past.

"We've always been told to respect white people. We have to live with these people all our lives. We have to get along with them."

Some people in the valley feel that education is the same as assimilation. These girls don't agree. "Indian kids that assimilate start early. They are nasty, mean to other Indian kids. They are (only) nice to their white friends."

Some parents are afraid university will lead to assimilation. The girls' parents taught them, "Learn the white way but apply it to the Indian people in your community so you don't lose affiliation with Indian people." Their father is very traditional, "Your people come first."

Jeanine worried that she would be treated differently when she came back from university. "Everyone studies you when you come back from being away at school. People look at you as a visitor, as if you don't belong in the community anymore." Her parents made her watch how she talked to people, so she didn't "talk down to them." Now she feels she can talk comfortably to Band members or to professors. She's grateful her parents emphasized that point with her.

Wendy Terbasket

Wendy, the youngest daughter, came into the room and joined the interview about half way through. She is shorter and slighter than her sisters. She was wearing large glasses and her long hair hung loose. She wore snug pants and a loose cardigan sweater. Wendy had a degree in Creative Writing from the University of Victoria, in Victoria, B.C.

They agreed that there is some conflict between their parents about the purpose of an education. Their father's attitude is, "You get educated to help your people." Their mother believes, "You get educated for yourself, to be successful." They find their dad easier to get along with now that he doesn't work so hard. They feel closer to him. "His attitude has changed, he sees things differently now." "Do what you want, " is his advice regarding Jeanine's jitters about being a lawyer. Her mother's attitude is, "You'll get over it." The girls feel that their parents measure success differently. "Mom was influenced by her mother, who was half white, and by her white stepfather. She is more materialistic, as white people are. Financial security means success to her. Lauren is very much like that. Mom has a lot of white values. This caused a clash with our father's cultural values when we were growing up." They describe both parents as `bullheaded.' "That's where Kathy gets it from."

Their parents didn't tell the girls what they could or couldn't do. They didn't tell them not to drink, but said, "You'll have to pay in the end." The girls learned from their own mistakes. Their parents didn't demand, but would say, "I want you to...," or "It would be nice if you did..." regarding school, alcohol, etc. The girls claim they learned from their parents how to manipulate their parents and each other. They describe Karen, their oldest sister, as being like their dad - "community oriented, and a workaholic. She sacrifices her family. There's a good housing program (on the reserve) because Karen works well with D.I.A. (Department of Indian Affairs). Karen's a good lobbyist and fundraiser for other causes as well."

The girls confided that their lives are very enmeshed, but that they give each other room if they need it. They feel they are not judgmental of each other, and are willing to accept others (boyfriends) into the family. They have learned to be diplomats. "That comes from politics."

Wendy expressed the feeling that her upbringing had been somewhat different from that of her older sisters, "Mom went back to work, therefore, there were few guidelines or rules for me when I was growing up." She says she just got to know her father in the last year, since she moved to live with him when her mother remarried.

Throughout the interview with the three girls the door would open periodically, and either Lauren or Kathy would look in, wanting to know how much longer we would be. They were anxious to get started for the pow-wow in Coeur d' Alene. The girls commented, "They wouldn't rush for us. We don't have to rush for them," and they refused to be hurried. Their father was already at the pow-wow and they were going to meet him. They were going mainly as spectators, rather than participants, and were staying for only one night.

The interview ended when lunchtime was announced. It was explained to me that the office is always locked from 12:00 to 1:00 while everyone goes for lunch.

Karen Terbasket

I had an appointment at 1:30 to interview Karen, John's oldest daughter. She is in charge of Capital Management and Housing for the Similkameen Band. In her position she lobbies for money and handles the funds for housing, day care, economic development and the core administration budget. After graduating from secondary school, she completed a course in Early Childhood Education.

Karen, attractively dressed in a skirt and blouse, directed me to her office, the second one down the left-hand hallway. When I commented on how nice the offices were, Karen explained that they had recently been painted and updated. They were a bright creamy white. She said they used to be very dark.

As we started to talk, it was obvious that she had thought very seriously about the problems of the Lower Similkameen people, including the educational problems. Karen was aware of the shortcomings of education in the valley. As she outlined some of the problems, I realized that she didn't recognize how well the kids were doing compared to Native kids in other places.

Karen was concerned that boys were more likely to be put into Special Education/vocational courses at school, such as mechanics, woodworking, and the forestry technical program, rather than into academic programs. "The valley is a labor intensive area. There are work opportunities in forestry, ranching, and fruit growing. Therefore boys tend to drop out after high school rather than going into postsecondary training. There is little opportunity to advance; little future in the community. It is becoming more of a retirement community. There is a lot of building going on. People are moving from the city, having kids; young people are moving back to Keremeos with their families.

"Girls are pushed into more discipline, to be more responsible. Many of the girls are reluctant to leave the community. A girl used to go to the boy's reserve to live when they married. In this valley, the opposite is now happening." (This situation is creating a need for more jobs in the valley.)

Karen brought up some of her other concerns. "In the last few years people are more aware of the importance of completing their education while funding is available (before the dissolution of the Department of Indian Affairs, through which the government currently provides funding). People are aware that funding may soon dry up." Lillian

Gottfriedsen, Education Coordinator for the Band, recently told Karen that many members of the Similkameen Band have applied for post-secondary education. Some have applied for courses that are only a few months long, others are degree programs at universities. Karen explained that Lillian Gottfriedsen is a participant in the inter-ministry committee in the Similkameen Valley, which is made up of representatives from Ministry of Social Services and Housing, probation office, Royal Canadian Mounted Police and Native social development committee. Lillian is in contact with all students from preschool to postsecondary, and is in charge of education funding and reporting to the government. She is also a member of the Tribal Council Education Committee, an organization representing all the Okanagan Indian Bands.

Karen told me that when she was in high school she was streamed into a general program even though she could have handled the academic courses. At the time her parents were so busy in the administration office that Karen felt pressured to help at home with the younger children. Therefore she didn't worry about her own academic future. She said Lauren had felt the same pressure, but was bright and went through the academic program. She smiled when she said the reason she stayed in school instead of quitting when she wanted to was because she was "too nervous of my parents." She said she was given a lot of support by the school staff when she got discouraged. The teachers provided her with assignments and she was able to complete her final examinations.

A concern of Karen's is that teaching seems to be "more of a job to teachers now, than a `calling' as it used to be. Teachers used to put in more time and effort." She feels the kids lose out. Two new positions were instituted at the high school for Native students: Home School Coordinator and Counsellor/Tutor. Karen thinks the results have been disappointing because the teachers seem to have cut back on the tutoring and counselling they used to do. Now "the negative aspects are shuffled onto the people in these positions and they are left to do the trouble shooting.

The Bands pushed for these two positions so the quality of the kids' education would be improved." Karen worries that the kids' skills are still low so "they are assigned, rather than promoted, to higher grades." The positions have not accomplished what the Native people hoped for. She worries that some kids are being "pushed through the system."

Karen told me that when her sister, Lauren, volunteered to help at the Cawston School, she found that some teachers called students "special needs kids" or "problem kids" because they wouldn't always do as they were told. Lauren found them to be just bright kids. She said if you got them interested, they were very keen. The longer Lauren worked there, the more of these "problem" students (Native and nonNative) were sent to her. Lauren, being bright herself, felt a common bond with them.

According to Karen, parent groups, Native and nonNative, are very active in the valley. There are a lot of parent volunteers in the schools. When positions for teachers' assistants were instituted in the schools a few years ago they were filled by former volunteers.

Changing topics, Karen explained that, historically, there is a different relationship between Indians and whites in the Similkameen than in other communities. For example, during the Depression, the Native people with big ranches helped other people. This may have helped to influence attitudes.

Karen lent me copies of the <u>Community Profile of the Similkameen Native Community: 1985</u> and an updated profile for 1985-1995. The books contained demographic data valuable to my study.

John Terbasket

After Karen and I had talked for about two hours, someone called on the intercom and said her dad was in the office if I wanted to talk to him. When I went out to the waiting room, John came over with a big smile on his face. He shook my hand. He was as slim as ever and looked just the same, except his greying hair was long and caught back in a ponytail.

He walked with a slight stoop that hadn't been there before. "It's been a long time," he said.

John got a key and unlocked the office next to Karen's at the end of the hall. He ushered me into the chair by the desk and sat down in a chair near the wall. I described my study to him and, without any preamble, he began giving me his views on Native education in the Similkameen Valley. I wrote as fast as I could for an hour and a half. John seldom paused for breath. I wished I had suggested using the tape recorder that I carried with me.

John feels that the history of the Similkameen people has had a strong influence on the present. "When the white men came, they introduced horses. The Indians adapted quickly to horses and began raising them. Around Hedley there were a thousand horses, and around the border area at Chopaka there were a thousand horses. One year some Russians came and bought about three hundred head of horses. They made sure they got the best ones by testing them in the corral. Horses became an economic base.

"Then came cattle. `Indian' Edwards had a herd of a thousand head of cattle. He would work for white people for small wages and a few head of cattle. He gradually built up his herd. Because of problems with rustlers, he sold his herd and rebuilt it to a thousand head three times.

"People in this valley have always had good work habits. This has continued over the years. Parents' work habits have rubbed off on the kids." John feels this has a lot to do with kids being successful at school.

"The success of the cow herds made a difference, too. During the Depression, a lot of white people came from the prairies and worked for the Indian ranchers just for their board. They were farmers who went broke on the prairies." They stayed for about ten years. During that time they influenced Indian people's ideas about the importance of education.

"During the 1950s alcohol became a problem. When the Indians took over the Indian Office (Similkameen Indian Administration Office) in the early 1970s, they tried to do economic development first; but found they needed social development first because of alcoholism. So they worked on social development. Now they are starting on economic development because of the need for jobs for Band members. "In the last ten years we've discovered we can't leave our culture behind. We're concentrating more on that. The En'owkin Centre in Penticton, and NVIT in Merritt both have a great success rate with Native students. They are starting to include culture in the curriculum. A lot of ceremonies and cultural activities are coming back. Pow-wows provide a place for social exchange." It became apparent to me that people in the community hold differing views on the importance of traditional culture in contemporary life. John is a very strong advocate of reviving the traditional culture.

"Residential schools hurt the Indians. They tried to change family patterns. A lot of kids that came out didn't know how to parent (their own kids), therefore there's a need for social development now. It took fifteen to twenty years to rebuild families. It takes two or three generations to cure the problems. Organized religion really hurt us, even though the intention was good. Residential schools broke down communication between parents and kids. Kids in residential schools were whipped for speaking their language." John explained that he lost his language at school, as many kids did. Loss of the language broke down the social structure. "Education is really weak in the northern areas of the province because the social structure was destroyed by residential schools. Only a few of us in this valley went to residential schools. The priest and the police came to the reserve at one time, loaded up the kids and hauled them away. Some families in Penticton got out guns and said, `No way you'll take my kids.' A few families were able to get away with that. The first couple of years this happened. Then parents accepted it because they had no idea how to stop it. `The law was the law.' Most families didn't speak much English, so they couldn't defend themselves. Barney's grandfather, John Fall Allison, was white. So that group spoke quite a bit of English.

"A lot of kids went to residential school for a lot of years, sometimes seven or eight years. Some went for only two or three years. The food wasn't fit for human consumption." John remembers when he was at the school in Cranbrook, "Kids would steal frozen turnips from the cellar in the middle of the night to stop their hunger pains. Five and six year olds really suffered being away from their parents for ten months of the year. We're fortunate here. We're quite a ways from any residential schools so not many people went. The towns that were close to a school, like Williams Lake and Kamloops, more kids went."

John explained that organized religion and traditional culture are starting to clash in the valley. "We recognize this as growing pains. We think success is going to come when the young people realize where they come from. Tremendous changes will take place with Indians in the next ten years." John met with the bishop to tell him the Catholic Church needs to get involved in helping bring about the changes because of the damage the church clergy have done. He suggested that perhaps they can help with money and/or political pressure on the government.

"Culture is helping young kids to identify who they are. The most trouble is with kids and adults who have rejected organized religion and have nothing to take its place." John clarified for me, "This is just our culture group that feels this way, not all the Indians in the valley.

"It's important not to be too materialistic. That has hurt the environment by destroying the forests, etc. Money has become more important than families. We realize we've done a lot of damage to our lands because of money. Now we're getting closer to Mother Earth. We have a lot of struggles to get back our culture. The church made the mistake of leaving culture out. Sweat lodges and pipe ceremonies are coming back. Some of the Indians are thinking about building a spiritual center here where people can come for six weeks, six months, one week, etc., for basic spiritual training. It would be up Ashnola at the pow-wow grounds." John feels this will strengthen students to do even better in education, if they attend for a period of time before they go off to school.

He said that cultural awareness in this valley started about 1972. John first attended a pow-wow when he was in his thirties. The music really touched him. At first it was just the dress and dances, then he realized there was a spiritual part to it. "Some of the people are getting deeper into spiritual things." John is comfortable with this. "It's like some people are priests and bishops in the Catholic Church. A lot of us, including myself, want to stay at the basics and help others with those." John feels that involvement in traditional religion has influenced his daughters and others and has led to them doing better in education.

"Young people are looking to us as elders, but we're still `kids' at the spiritual level so we're bringing other people to help us.

"Residential school confused a lot of people regarding who they are." John gave an example of a Band that is making a lot of money, "…the material side looks good but the social development is not there." They have problems with drugs and alcohol.

According to John, some people in the Similkameen Band are thinking of taking over their own education program and building their own school. "They think that by doing this they can help kids realize what they really want to be, not what their parents push them into. We realize a lot of teachers are just `teaching for the bucks,' so kids don't get that much attention. There are lots of problems in education: too much attention on success, on grades. Kids may do their best but still be considered failures. The Band would like to start with a school for kindergarten to grade five or six .Then work their way up. It would be more into culture. Indians are more outdoor people. We would change the curriculum to more on-the-job training to get kids interest, as well as teaching the basics." John sees the school as also being an economic base for the Band, by providing jobs for twenty or thirty people. It would be built up at Ashnola near the pow-wow grounds, "an area that is spiritual and unpolluted." The curriculum would tie spiritual teachings in with basic education; for example, they would teach the importance of land, trees and water, and the importance of looking after them. Elders would be asked to teach spiritual values in the school.

John thinks the Indians will eventually go back to traditional ways. This will help to get away from so many political decisions. The best people will do the job. There will be no competition for positions. Everything will be decided by consensus of the people. People will be trained for lifetime positions, e.g., spiritual and political leaders. John explained that a lot of Bands are looking at the spiritual/cultural aspect of their development. The Merritt area has well educated leaders, but is not yet looking at traditional ways.

When John was young, the old people told him there would be a traditional revival, but he didn't believe them. "The elders said that the main goal of the Indians is to look after the land. The traditional way is that no one should be put on a pedestal, but everyone should try to be in the middle of the pack, quietly influencing others."

John believes that today the worst part isn't just surviving because of alcoholism, like it was when he was a kid. His mother died when he was young. He used to get on a horse and try to decide which neighbor's house to go to to eat. He'd try not to go to anyone's house too often. In 1972 about 98% of the Native adults in the valley were alcoholics according to John and other Band members. John went to a reunion a couple years ago, and three-quarters of the people his age weren't around. They had died of alcoholism. Now only about half of the Band members are alcoholics. John sees this as an indication that the social programs have made a difference.

John and I were interrupted shortly after 4:30 when someone started announcing that the office was closing. Outside the building, John and Karen and I talked for a few minutes. I noticed that Karen and her father seemed to be on the same wave length about several things they discussed that related to the Band.

I thanked them for their help, then drove back to Hedley mulling over the events of the day.

Philip

When I got to the Band office the next morning Carol and Kathy, the secretaries, said it would be a few minutes before I could interview either of them. Frank, Karen's husband, was in a meeting. She had suggested the day before that he would be a good person for me to talk to. "I don't know if he'll talk to you. He's awfully quiet, but I'll ask him."

I sat down in one of the straight-backed chairs in the waiting area and started reviewing my notes from the day before. A young couple sitting there kept casting furtive glances at me, apparently curious as to why I was hanging around the office.

I noticed there were various Native publications on some shelves near me. Philip, a Frenchman who was hired by the Band because of his expertise in research, rushed passed about then. I had noticed that Philip was always in a rush. No wonder he was so slim.

"Philip!" He stopped and turned toward me. (In his name the final i is pronounced like e in "deep.") "Philip, is there a library here?"

"If you are interested in books and files, you can come upstairs with me." I noted his accent.

I followed him up a set of stairs that were hidden by a wall behind where I'd been sitting. At the top of the stairs was a huge room with a rounded ceiling. The room held a museum containing the beginnings of an artifact collection of the Indians of the Similkameen Valley. Reluctantly I hurried across the museum, trying to keep sight of Philip. He had disappeared through a door at the back of the room.

The room I entered seemed to be another well kept secret. No one had mentioned to me that there was a collection of books or that there were boxes and boxes of files waiting to be explored. Vaguely in the back of my mind I recalled Slim saying, "If you want to see the files, ask Philip. He knows them better than anyone." There was an older model IBM computer on the large desk. Philip told me this was a quiet place for him to work.

He started rushing around, pulling papers from here and there and handing them to me. "Here, sit here," he said, clearing a pile of books off a chair.

I sat down and began leafing through the papers. Without warning, the chair toppled to the floor. The whole right side of it broke off. I was mortified, sitting there amidst the pieces.

Philip, also, was obviously embarrassed.

I scrambled to my feet.

Bringing me another chair from the far side of the desk, he frowned, "Hopefully this one will be strong enough." Then, with his back to me, he busied himself at the bookshelves for several minutes.

Philip was very helpful as he dug out several books and files he thought might be important to my study. He suggested other titles for me to get from the library, and he shared a file from a report he was currently writing. "Would this be of any help to you?"

I realized that a large section on demographic data in the file would be very valuable to me.

"I'll take this down and make you a copy," he said.

When I started to express how grateful I was, he shook his head, "You don't have to thank me. Slim told me I was to help you. It's part of my job."

He returned a few minutes later with the photocopied material. "I'll have to leave you now," he said. "I have a meeting. You are welcome to stay and go through things yourself."

I was ecstatic. I wished I had days to spend in that room. A few minutes later Philip returned with a box of files from the education office. "I gave these to Lillian (the Education Coordinator) to look at, but she's not here today. You might as well see if there is anything."

I found three or four books that looked particularly useful and several pamphlets and reports. I'd been there for about three-quarters of an hour when the light began to flicker. I knew I didn't want to be alone in that windowless upstairs room if the lights went out. Grasping my treasures, I went back downstairs.

Frank Qualtier

Karen was watching for me. "Frank's here now." She ushered me into the office where I'd talked to her dad the day before. She returned almost immediately with a tall, slim young man. His eyes had a watchful, thoughtful expression.

"This is Frank," she said. There was something special about the way she said it, almost bashfully. Her cheeks glowed pink and her eyes had a shine I hadn't seen there before.

Karen left us, and I explained the nature of my study. Frank said Karen had told him a bit about it. During our conversation he was quite open and told me some very private and painful happenings in his life.

Frank's father died when he was four years old. Two years later he and his brother Harry (Harp) were sent to residential school in Cranbrook for two years. This was just before the school was closed. Frank remembers that there was a lot of harsh treatment at the school. Shortly after he arrived he "got strapped on a false excuse." He felt sure that the nuns knew he hadn't broken a window but they wanted to show their power over him. There were three departments of boys at the school and separate departments of girls. The boys weren't allowed near the girls at any time, even if they were their sisters. If one boy got in trouble, all the boys in his department were punished. Some of the punishments Frank remembers besides the strap, were having to stand in cold showers, doing without supper and not getting to watch movies or television. He remembers that the food at the school was not great. He lost most of his language because he was forbidden to speak it while he was there.

After the school was closed, Frank and Harp were put in a foster home for five years with an abusive, alcoholic couple. They were in the small town of Westbank, sixty-five miles northeast of Keremeos. During that time they were subjected to fighting, name calling, and prejudice. Twice they ran away, both times making it back to Keremeos. The first time, when they went into a store to ask for directions to their grandmother's, the police were notified and they were returned to the foster home. A year later, they determined to try again. This time they took their dog with them, walking along the highway, taking cover in ditches and behind bushes whenever a car approached. By the time they got to Summerland, a distance of twenty-five miles, it was dark. When they saw the lights of a car approaching, the boys ran to hide in the ditch at the edge of the road. Their dog, perhaps confused by the car lights, ran first to one side of the road and then the other. The car hit the dog, killing it instantly. Before Frank could stop him, Harp ran to help their pet.

The driver of the car tried to comfort them. He asked if he could drive them home. Frank accepted the offer, saying it was "a ways down the road" to their grandmother's house. He kept giving the man directions until they finally reached the Chopaka Reserve south of Keremeos. This time the boys were allowed to remain.

They went to live with John and Delphine Terbasket. Frank found the school in Keremeos much better than those he was used to. There was no prejudice. He was in the top seven or eight of the class, and didn't feel he was treated any differently than anyone else. He liked English and Social Studies, except he was a bit "teed off" that history was taught from a white man's point of view. "Sports helped to keep me in school. I was involved in basketball, volleyball and enjoyed track-and-field activities: long distance running, shotput, discus, and high jump. In grade twelve I tied for top athlete of the school."

Frank believes that proper parenting is important in encouraging kids to carry on with their education. The people who told him that education was important, besides his school counsellor John Drossos, now retired but still a great favorite in the valley, were John and Delphine Terbasket and his grandmother, Julia Qualtier. The message he got from these people was "If you want to do ranching or work in the orchards, that's okay. Otherwise get an education."

Traditional religion was part of Frank's early life. As a young child and as a teenager, he used to do a lot of "sweats" (a traditional religious ceremonial cleansing performed in a small sweathouse built for the purpose). The sweats gave him strength.

Frank's experiences in residential school, and in the foster home have had a lasting influence on him. It's important to him that his family is well taken care of. This helps him stay away from alcohol. Although he drank heavily at one time, when he started getting into serious fights he quit drinking. That was more than ten years ago. He has since taken courses so that he can counsel others on their problems with alcohol. Frank enjoyed the opportunity he had to fill in at the band office for a year as a counsellor. He has been farming for a few years and works seasonally for the forestry. He has recently agreed to coach basketball for boys thirteen to seventeen years old. He likes the fact that a lot of young boys come to his house and treat him as a substitute father. He thinks that it might help to have a fathers group to plan sports activities, etc. Also, to discuss the best way to resolve social problems, such as situations their kids get into. "There's a lot of guys at home because of the lack of work, especially during the winter." Frank feels that there needs to be more planning regarding jobs and volunteer work. Most of the guys his age see their wives as equals so they are willing to pitch in and help out at home with their kids.

I was surprised and delighted with how talkative Frank was, especially considering Karen's warning that he might not say much. By the end of the interview I was a staunch admirer of his, very impressed with his ability to have survived so many calamities.

Just as we were finishing someone called on the intercom to say that Barney, the chief of the Lower Similkameen Band, was in the office. I was very anxious to talk to him.

Chief Barney Allison

Barney was standing by the counter in the outer office. He shook my hand and gave me a warm welcome. We sat down together in the waiting room. Barney's nephew, August, was also in the office. I presumed he was waiting for Barney. I was surprised that Augie didn't speak to me or acknowledge my presence. When I had met him at a wedding on the Chopaka Reserve a year and a half earlier, he had given me a big hug and been very glad to see me. After Barney and I had been talking for about forty minutes, Augie jumped up from where he was sitting on the other side of the waiting room, rushed across the room with a big smile and shook my hand in welcome. "I didn't realize it was you!" he apologized.

This incident made me realize how difficult it would be for me to break the ice and get people to feel comfortable enough to confide in me, if they didn't already know me. If I was a stranger attempting this project, I probably would have had to move to the valley and stay for many months getting to know the people. Still, I doubt that they would have been as open with me, even then, as they were on my third day back in the valley.

Barney has been chief of the Lower Similkameen Band for twenty-three years. He was a student in the night school class I taught on the reserve twenty years earlier. Teaching that class forged a strong bond between me and many members of the Similkameen Band. It is because of that that the adults and elders remember me as well as they do and are encouraging the younger adults to participate in my study.

Barney feels that integration is a key to the success rate of Native students in the valley. "Integration has always been good here. This has always been a busy place for Indians going up and down the valley from Chopaka to Hedley. Years ago there were not too many white kids. That helped integration; everybody knew everybody."

Regarding residential schools, Barney remembers, "Catholic priests tried to force kids to go to residential school, but the parents wouldn't listen. The Indians were very good church goers. There was nothing else to do anyway (socially). They would often go to church even if there was no priest."

Barney first went to school in a small wooden structure a mile or so across the American border in Washington. He used to ride from the Chopaka Reserve with some of the other kids everyday on horseback. A few years earlier his older sisters had gone to school in a log building about half a mile further south. After that Barney spent one year at Kamloops Residential School, but refused to go back. "They almost starved me." Anyone seeing Barney's ample figure would know that wouldn't set well with him. His family then built a house across the river on the Upper Similkameen Reserve and he went to school at Hedley. He explained, "My dad and Slim's dad were brothers. We lived as much at Hedley as at Chopaka. The Indians rode up and down the valley those days. There were no trucks to haul horses. I must have rode that trip at least fifty times" (a distance of 30 miles.)

Barney explained that his wife, Margaret, had gone to the Omak Residential School in Washington state for several years, although she didn't like it. Her brother, Billy, was allowed to attend the "white school" near Keremeos, even though he couldn't speak English. "That was around 1900." Barney quoted a chief he had heard speak at a meeting, "You have to be strong to have survived residential school." Barney agrees. "They were starving us in those schools."

Since the early 1900s the Similkameen Indians have been well-to-do. According to Barney, "They helped one another by working for one another and paying off in cattle or horses. There were thousands of cattle and horses. All the Indians had gardens and root cellars in the Similkameen Valley. They put up hay with horses. It was a good way to live. Today no one has gardens. They hunted deer, boned and dried the meat, and put it in sacks for the winter. Now they hardly hunt. Today Indians settle for bologna and wieners from Super Valu. You can't blame the Indians for the deer population disappearing."

Regarding wealth among Native families, Barney reminisced, "There used to be twenty or thirty families owned cattle. Then when liquor opened up, many families drank up their cattle." About ten families now have the same number of cattle, around a thousand head, as were owned by twenty to thirty families years ago. Barney would like to see more families start cattle herds again. One problem he sees is that, "Young people want to borrow forty-five to fifty thousand dollars to buy cattle." Barney doesn't believe in this. "Pay as you go. Add one or two cattle a year.

"The government wanted to control the Crown ranges (government owned land) where the Indians ran their horses. The government started saying there were too many horses. They began paying five dollars for the ears from a horse, for people shooting horses on Crown land. Hundreds of horses were destroyed. That caused a lot of hard feelings when people shot horses for bounty money. One man (a bounty hunter) had his horse shot right out from under him. When he complained, he was warned, "Next time you'll be the one that gets shot." After that cattle were put on Crown ranges.

In 1937 Native people started paying range fees on Crown land. The federal government charged them thirty-five cents a head for cattle. Now people on the Lower Similkameen Reserve pay ten dollars a head every year, for a thousand head of cattle. Barney's response is, "Far as I can see, I've been paying range fees on my own land for fifty years." "By the 1920s the Similkameen Indians had enough money to start buying cars for transportation. They bought them from Burr Motors in Princeton. Burr was a blacksmith at Hedley. He owned the Williams ranch near the Golden Dawn Cafe. Then he started Burr Motors in Princeton."

Barney feels that sports have contributed a lot to integration in the community. There are two or three ball clubs and two annual rodeos. The rodeos on the Chopaka Reserve developed gradually. "It started with kids first communion at church. Then we added a picnic. Then started a small rodeo. It's lots of work. There's a bigger rodeo now. We used to pass the hat - got seventy to ninety dollars. This year we charged and got several thousand dollars. There were two hundred and fifty entries, from Fort St. John to Omak and further south. There was no limit to the number of entries because there was lots of stock - horses from Penticton and Williams Lake. We have to pay for them now." The rodeo takes place on Easter weekend, lasting for three days.

Barney and I were still talking when someone announced that the office was closing for lunch. We went outside together. He seemed very interested in my study and willing to help. He told me to talk to his daughters Nan and Carol who work in the Band office.

Nancy (Nan) Allison

When I went back to the office after lunch Nan, Barney's daughter, was behind the counter. I asked if she'd have time to talk to me. She took me into one of the back offices and talked to me for three hours. Almost everyone I interviewed in an office motioned me to the chair at the desk, and they took a less comfortable seat. I puzzled over whether they were giving me the most comfortable seat, or if it was because I obviously planned to take notes?

Nan is the fourth of Barney's six daughters. She is very serious in her concerns about the young people in the valley and has dedicated many years in an effort to see that their needs are met. She told me that she was strongly influenced by three role models, her favorite aunts - Mary Allison (Mrs. Bobby), Mary Allison (Mrs. Charlie) and Ramona Allison-Heinrich. She remembers their kindness and has tried to teach that to the kids she has worked with.

Nan has legitimate reasons for believing that sports have made a valuable contribution to the success of students in the valley. She dropped out of school in grade eleven to continue developing recreational programs for the kids from the Lower Similkameen Band. Until then there were recreational programs for adults but none for kids. Nan had no training; she built on what she knew. She managed boys and girls basketball, softball and rodeo events. These three activities kept the kids occupied year round. Starting in 1974 Nan managed the girls sports for fourteen years and the boys for five years. Although she has many wonderful memories of her work with the girls, she still has regrets about giving up management of the boys group.

"I worked with the same eighteen boys for five years, managing the team and finding them coaches. They ranged in age from eight to twelve years when I started. I reluctantly gave up managing the team when some of the fathers started complaining that they didn't want their sons to have a female manager. They wanted the boys to have strong male role models so they took over management of the group. After six months they felt they had done their share. From then on the boys were left on their own, with no manager and no guidance. They even coached themselves. A couple of the boys would come to the girls' practices to share ideas with me about their basketball team. These two were always the leaders of the boys. Both of them are now coaches and leaders among the young men. Even after two years I wanted to start managing the boys again but I felt the fathers wouldn't accept it. To this day some of the boys think I deserted them and that I shouldn't have let them down." Nan feels the boys would have been more successful in school and would have become better role models for the younger boys if she had kept working with them and teaching them traditional values. Only six of the eighteen boys graduated from high school, compared to twenty-eight of the twenty-nine girls she worked with.

While managing the basketball teams, she did a lot of teaching of attitudes. She taught discipline, the meaning of authority, sportsmanship, sharing, etiquette, the importance of team work. She taught the kids that it was important when playing in other towns, if billeted out, to show proper manners and to be good ambassadors for their community. She emphasized the importance of never being lazy.

Nan recruited Agnes Bush, a girls' physical education teacher who was retired from the high school in Keremeos, to start the girls out in basketball and help teach them etiquette. For two winters Mrs. Bush coached the girls at the Cawston Hall every week. She taught them: "Winner's never quit and quitters never win," and "We're only as strong as our weakest player." When I visited Mrs. Bush she shared with me the attendance records she had kept of the girls' basketball practices and a beautiful Valentine card she still treasures, signed by all the girls on the team.

Rob Hughes was another coach Nan arranged for the girls. Unintentionally, he modelled for them the acceptability of a male playing "Mr. Mom." An unemployed teacher at the time, he stayed home while his artist wife worked. He was the girls' coach when they won the championship. Nan told me there are now about ten Mr. Moms in the Lower Similkameen Band. She sees this as a positive sign of change. She feels the men wouldn't have done this a few years ago.

The girls were eight to twelve years old when Nan started managing the team. Some of the mothers resented her, saying she was "too young to be taking the girls around." Nan agrees that she was too young. Although there were usually about twenty on the team, over the fourteen year period she worked with nearly thirty different girls. Each year the same girls joined the team with only a few variations. Sometimes one would drop out then start again the next season. She worked with them right up through the championships.

When Nan first started there was a recreation club attended by about twenty adult Band members. They said that if the kids wanted money for recreation, they should help fund raise. Soon most of the adults dropped out, complaining that too much of the money was going to basketball. After that, the kids formed `The Basketball Club.'

Nan pushed the girls on the basketball team to get their education as she had been pushed by some of her relatives. She had realized too late that they had been right about the importance of an education. She always meant to go back and finish but there never seemed to be time. Nan talked to her dad, who looked ahead to when government funding for Native education might stop. Barney told her, "If you kids make it, the Indian people will make it. This generation is the elastic."

She encouraged the kids to get educated in order to take over important positions in the Band that would be needed when funding was no longer available. She is sometimes "afraid they may get over-educated so they can't communicate with other people in the Band." She tells them when they come home they should be sure to contact the main households, so they don't lose contact with the Band members. According to Nan, there are seven main households.

While I was there, Nan asked her sister Carol to help her figure out how many of the kids in The Basketball Club had graduated. They were surprised when they realized that only one of the girls hadn't graduated. According to Nan, "The girls grew up with a strong self-image, good self-esteem." She thinks this will carry over into their lives, and that it will affect how they raise their children. She believes that they will raise their boys and girls more equally. The result should be that in the future boys will be given more responsibility, and more encouragement to do well.

When one of the boys from The Basketball Club died in a car accident in 1977, "The boys group sort of fell apart. They put everything down for a year, then never picked it up again." Nan feels there was not enough social development in the community to help them deal with the grief. They weren't able to grieve and recover. As children the boys as well as the girls were always taught to be strong, "Don't cry."

Seven years later, when a girl from the Club committed suicide, the girls didn't play anymore basketball that year. Nan, who had taken some courses in social development, was able to help them deal with their grief. They recovered in time to play the next year. Nan believes this shows there had been social growth in the community.

Nan is concerned that in grade eight some kids, especially boys, are shuffled into Special Education classes. "The kids don't mind, until about grade eleven, because it's easier. Then they discover they can't get as many credits as kids in the mainstream. It's too late then to go back into the regular stream of education. Some kids graduate from Special Ed but without many useable skills." Not as many girls have ended up in Special Ed. Because older parents associate school with residential school, they tend not to want to get involved in their kids' schooling. This has resulted in many kids being shuffled into Special Ed and parents not complaining. The parents' education committee is starting to try to keep that from happening. Nan told me that the Band is very supportive of the students. If they hear of a teacher that shows signs of being prejudiced, as has happened on rare occasions in the past, the Band Council will take their concerns to the School Board. The School Board has demonstrated support for their concerns.

In addition to managing basketball teams, Nan was active in the organization and management of softball teams and rodeo participation, always with the same kids. These three sports created year round activities. Nan spent about three days a week on recreation - getting people to maintain the grounds, fund raising, managing teams, etc. She did this for about ten years for no salary. Then, when the band was better organized and started having more money, she started getting a salary. After fourteen years, Nan decided she should get a paying job and do something for herself, so she quit managing the group. By then several girls were college age and were going away to school. They still get together for games when enough of them are home. Seven of them are now coaches for sports teams.

Men and women who belonged to the Basketball Club get together every couple of months for communication group meetings. They discuss problems and things they are concerned about including, "Are we doing what we said we would do when we `grew up'?" This group has agreed to rid itself of the family feuds traditional among three factions of the Band. Their mottoes are, "Let's have a truce in this generation," and "We should be fighting for each other, instead of fighting with each other."

Discipline is another popular topic. They discuss the strict discipline some of them received from their parents, such as hard lickings and why some of them now do the same thing to their children. Through workshops and discussions they are realizing that, unconsciously, they are beating their parents rather than their children. The communication group is helping them understand why they do some of the things they do.

As I interviewed the young women of the Band, I became aware of a subtle thread that appeared in several conversations. When I asked Nan about it, she explained that the women refer to themselves, unofficially, as the `Similkameen Women's Screening Committee.' They screen the new wives and other women that the men bring into the valley. Some of the men blame their marriage breakups on this `screening committee'. She gave an example of a man who has been married for twelve years. Only during the past year have the women started to accept his wife. The men tend to be more accepting of newcomers. Men brought into the valley by the women are usually well accepted by men and women. Nan thinks this is partly because the women take their men and introduce them fairly soon to the main families. "The men tend to hide their women until everyone knows about them from gossip." "The community is very close knit. The valley women tend to be strong and to only accept strong women." Carol told me later that during a recent meeting the men had voiced their concerns about this practice. Since then, "The women are trying not to do any more screening."

Traditional religion was strong in Nan's family because of her mother's traditional upbringing. Margaret gave her six daughters medicine baths in the bathhouse down by the creek about every two weeks while they were growing up, even in the winter. Margaret gathered herbs, boiled them and put them into heated water from the creek. When pouring water over the girls to rinse them, she would pray for them to be strong. She knew they would need to be strong when they grew up, prepared for the difficulties of life. Nan feels sure that if her mother had had sons, she would have also given them medicine baths.

Traditional religion is quite widely practiced today, though not openly, by the people in the valley. It has been carried on throughout the generations. Many people practice traditional religion as well as Catholic. Nan thinks people forty years old and younger are leaning more toward traditional religion than toward the Catholic.

She told me that, traditionally, each family had their own medicines. Her family belonged to the "river and tree families." Other groups were the "sage families" and the "stone families." Nan remembers burning her arm when she was up in Ashnola as a child. The woman she was visiting put a poultice on the burn. The ingredients were basically salt and fat. When Nan got home, her mother told her that was not the right thing to put on a burn. Margaret replaced the poultice with one made of bacon and something salty (basically fat and salt). Although each family group had their own medicines, Nan believes the basic ingredients were the same.

Ninety-five percent of Nan's generation never learned the Similkameen language, because their parents were punished for speaking it when in residential school. Many parents hesitated to teach their children something they might later be punished for. The Okanagan language, which has fewer sounds, has largely taken the place of the Similkameen language. The young people have not learned to speak Okanagan either.

Nan's openness during the interview allowed us to cover a wide range of topics. When she left she asked her sister Carol to come in. Carol and I talked for an hour, until the call came at 4:30 to close the office.

Carol Allison

Carol said her parents were responsible for her staying in school. "Dad said to get an education because we had the opportunity. (Her parents only went to around grade four or five.) Mom was the disciplinarian in our family. Dad was the softy."

I asked Carol about the influence of The Basketball Club on its members. "The girls pressured each other to stay in school. They tried to pressure the boys to keep going. It worked with six or seven of the boys that the girls stayed close to. In our age group, girls discipline each other "... regarding drugs, alcohol, etc. "We are close like sisters. When we were around fifteen to seventeen years old, we got into alcohol, not drugs. We stuck close to protect each other. Most of the girls quit drinking seven or eight years ago. Boys of that age got heavily into drugs and alcohol. Most of them still drink a lot, and a fair number still use marijuana. Some of them are becoming more conscious of being seen as role models, therefore more of them are giving up drugs and alcohol."

Carol couldn't recall any outstanding teacher. "A few strict teachers made you do your work. The fact that the teachers are fairly open (not prejudiced) helps a lot. You don't notice racism in this valley."

When asked about intermarriage, Carol observed, "There's not much intermarriage." After some reflection, she concluded, "There was one (mixed marriage) in 1979. Then there wasn't another one until 1989. Most girls don't consider white men as marriage partners but boys do consider white girls as marriage partners." Carol doesn't think this pressure comes from parents. "The girls haven't really talked about this. We've probably all dated nonIndians, but not seriously." She assured me that the children of mixed marriages are accepted as equals by the people in the Band.

During the course of our conversation Carol confirmed some of the things Nan had said to me. Referring to traditional religion, she said, "It was never given up by most of the families in the valley." She found her mother's herbs and legends strengthening. Legends were stories told to help people through the difficult times in their lives.

When we left the office, Barney was outside waiting for his daughters. He tapped me on the arm, shook my hand and wished me luck with my project, "In case I don't see you again for awhile."

Theresa Ann Terbasket

The next morning Theresa Ann Terbasket phoned before we left the house. Carrie said, "Lila wants to talk to you," and handed me the phone. Theresa Ann had been a student in the night school class I taught in Chopaka. She has taken a lot of schooling since then - training as a court support worker and as a linguistics teacher for the Okanagan language. Now she works as the Community Health Representative for the Band. I briefly outlined my project to her and Theresa Ann invited me to come and talk to her that morning at the Band Field Office in Cawston. She said she'd be there until noon.

I had a little trouble finding the Field Office, hidden away at the foot of the mountain on the Blind Creek Reserve. Eventually I sighted the two storey doublewide mobile structure. Next door to it was the Tee Pee Tot Day Care Centre, a modern one storey building.

Since no one was in the reception area, I called out a greeting, then continued on until I came to Theresa Ann's office. She stood behind a big desk, as tall as ever, dressed in slacks and a T-shirt. "This is where I hide out," she greeted me.

She told me that she enjoys her job but was disappointed when she had to move out of the main office in Keremeos. "They didn't think we got enough done in the main office, so they moved us down here. The truth is we don't get any more done here and it's not nearly as much fun. Once they proved that, I asked if they'd move us back again but they said no."

During our conversation Theresa Ann showed me the pictures on her office walls. There were pictures of her grandchildren, her children and various events in the valley. She pointed out her son, Michael, who was killed in a car accident in 1987. She said, "They had to fill the hall down Chopaka three times to feed the people that came to his funeral." She couldn't believe how many people from all over had known and cared for Michael. She tried to make a point of speaking to everyone who came to the funeral, to show her appreciation.

Theresa Ann described herself as having a dysfunctional family due to drinking. She eventually went to treatment at the Round Lake Centre "to clear out the garbage". In spite of the problems, four of her six children graduated from high school.

She has strong views on the differences between men and women in the valley. "Women have strong role models. They have been encouraged to do well. Men need different strokes to succeed. Men in this area were put on the back burner. Women suppressed the men."

Women never spoke out in public when Theresa Ann was growing up. When Henry Terbasket died, one of the leaders among the older men was asked to speak to the people because everyone was hurting. He didn't know what to say. He was hurting too. No one spoke. Theresa Ann thinks she might be able to speak if it happened now.

When she was growing up, "Women and girls had to work hard inside and outside. They did outside chores - wood and water, then still had to work indoors - washing clothes, cooking, cleaning. Men didn't work as hard - riding, mowing, haying, tractor driving. They became soft. Their morale was undermined by soft jobs. They did no inside work. The work ethic wasn't encouraged. Men and boys weren't encouraged to succeed. Skills men had traditionally, like hunting and fishing, became more like hobbies. Men were no longer respected for their accomplishments. Many men became alcoholics."

Women were able to take many of their traditional skills into the new way of life, therefore they kept their respect. Because of this, girls have had strong role models. Boys haven't. Theresa Ann feels this is still influencing boys in the valley. Girls are pushed to graduate. Boys aren't.

Theresa Ann gave me the example of how she raised her kids. "The girls had really strict rules they had to live by. The boys didn't. The girls had to have good marks in school. The boys didn't. The girls weren't encouraged to drink" (weren't discouraged either). Theresa Ann drank with her boys. If the girls went along they got the car keys (a responsibility, a trust). That's how she saw her uncles, and boy cousins raised - with few restrictions.

Boys were allowed to play but had to carry out responsibilities even if hung over, e.g., haying, driving cattle, etc. "That was my grandfather's rule." Men were "made fun of" for being hung over. This probably affected the boys, seeing the men ridiculed rather than respected.

"Recently, someone noticed boys were being less successful generally (than girls). We went through the records and discovered this was true. We began working on ways to encourage boys. Other Bands probably don't encourage either girls or boys. On some reserves the girls get pregnant at fourteen or fifteen years old. Therefore, they don't complete school. The girls here are programmed to succeed."

Theresa Ann had several phone calls during our interview. Not enough to be an interference, just enough to let me catch up on my note taking. The two girls working in the outer office left for lunch and returned while we continued our interview. About 2:30 I asked Theresa Ann if I could buy her lunch.

She accepted. First she phoned her niece Debbie to set up an interview for me. Debbie, the Home School Coordinator for the district, said to come that afternoon.

I followed Theresa Ann to the restaurant at the Cawston crossroads, about a ten minute drive. We had delicious homemade soup and turkey sandwiches. The restaurant was in a small store with a few tables and a counter with stools. The young man who waited on us was very friendly. Theresa Ann said their food was always good.

Debbie Crow

After lunch we said our goodbyes and I took the main road back to Keremeos. Half a block from the Similkameen Elementary Secondary School I parked beside the attractive A-frame house where Debbie, her husband, and two teenage sons live. The wind was blowing as I got out of the car, as it had been all day. I was conscious of my hair, clasped in the back by a barrette, being pulled loose and blown around. I had never quite come to terms with the wind in Keremeos.

Debbie opened the door with a smile, led me through her beautiful varnished wood kitchen, and invited me to sit on one of two couches facing each other in the living room. She made herbal tea, the first of two or three pots, then sat down on the couch opposite me. I felt somewhat at a disadvantage as the light through the window shades was in my eyes and her face was in shadow, making it hard to read.

Debbie was open, knowledgeable and forceful as she covered a wide range of topics. "There are strong women in this valley. When there's trouble in the schools, it's usually with the boys. Automation on ranches and in orchards has led to fewer jobs for men. There are few employment options - either go away or go on welfare. So there are few role models for the boys.

"Contact with white culture took away the nomadic way of life, large land base, men's need to protect others and gradually the need to hunt and fish." Debbie explained that some families adapted well, made good use of their land. They are the wealthier ones. Other families didn't adapt. Some of them have a large land base but they lease it out because they don't have the skills to ranch. Because of this, they earn only a small annual income from their land.

Debbie feels she and her brother were raised totally differently. Debbie was given lots of reponsibility, "female-type" chores. She was expected to earn her own money. Her brother had no responsibility. Her mother gave him money, even for dating. Her mother modelled "saint and victim." She worked hard in orchards and the packing house to support the family. I shook my head mentally, remembering how small Debbie's mother was.

Debbie thinks residential schools may be partly responsible for differences in the way boys and girls are raised. The girls were taught household skills by the nuns. They were taught to be busy, "never lazy," and to be subservient to the male population. The boys were taught whatever skills the priests thought were important, probably farming and gardening. When the girls became mothers, they taught their daughters as they had been taught. But the women, even today, "don't have a clue how to raise their boys. They don't know how to discipline them. They keep waiting for the men to take over the responsibility of raising the boys, but the men never have." Debbie's sons are fourteen and seventeen. Although she's done the best she could with them, she said if she'd had a daughter she would have been much stricter with her, would have expected her to do a lot of chores around the house at an early age.

Debbie's understanding is that before contact with Europeans, and during early contact times, men needed their time to prepare for hunting and battle, therefore they helped very little with domestic chores. "Now there's not so much outdoor work to do, still most men help very little with domestic chores."

She feels some boys may suffer from women being too strong, too aggressive - putting boys and men down. She believes that "women have evolved much further than men. The women will have to stop and wait for the men or help them catch up."

As a child Debbie remembers the women were always so busy. "They had a life, even if their husbands were alcoholics. In alcoholic families, it's usually the oldest girl that takes over the mother role." Probably more kids in the Similkameen have a "functional" mother than in most areas. That may account for some of the success of the students, especially the girls.

When I asked Debbie about the Similkameen Women's Screening Committee, her comment was, "Talk to women who have married into this valley. They go through a long period before they are accepted. The Committee doesn't exist officially, but unofficially it's very strong."

Commenting about reserves, Debbie said, "There's a sense of security about reserves. Your home on the reserve will never go away, it will always be there for you. She quoted a little slogan, "Home is home and always will be." Debbie is especially conscious of the security of the reserve because she lost her Native Indian status when she married Doug, who is white. She regained status for herself and her sons in 1986 through Bill C-31, which changed government regulations.

Respect for others was a traditional value of the Similkameen Indian culture. It is a value that has been retained. Debbie feels this is very important. "This makes it possible to get through to kids, especially if they've been taught to respect their elders. Kids respond to being respected, also they respond to honesty." Debbie found it much harder to get through to kids who moved to Keremeos from other districts. "Respect didn't work with them."

According to Debbie, only one or two teachers in the district stand out as prejudiced. "Often several kids are misbehaving, but a Native kid is singled out as the troublemaker." She and the other Native counsellor make a point of observing in the classroom, then encouraging parents to go in and see that teacher.

Debbie has a good working relationship with the teaching staff and the kids in the valley schools. She finds that "most of the kids have aspirations, some far beyond their abilities." She finds that some parents have "totally unrealistic aspirations for their kids. They say, `Go for it and get a better life.' "

Throughout the school year, the Band recognizes the importance of education on several occasions by honoring the students. At Christmas time they host a community potluck dinner for all the families. All interested teachers are welcome to attend. Debbie described it as being very positive. Last year she asked the teachers to provide her with a positive comment about each child. This Christmas, the focus was on post-secondary students. They were asked to speak on what they are doing at university. This was seen as providing good role models for younger students. In June a similar dinner is held to recognize students at the end of the school year. Last year the Band gave each student a T-shirt stating, "I'm the future of Similkameen." Each of the kids was asked to say, "When I grow up, I want to be...." The Chiefs and counsellors are asked to speak at the dinners. Barney Allison always speaks.

Debbie and I continued our conversation for so long that she invited me to take potluck with her family. Over a supper of homemade soup and hotdogs, Debbie and her husband Doug told me about kids their age that had been sent to residential school. When they returned after two or three years they seemed "different". How they were different was not explained. Debbie told how her grandfather, Tommy Terbasket, threatened the authorities with a gun when they came to take her father Ernie to residential school. He then sent Ernie to his grandparents where he felt he'd be safe.

Debbie and Doug shared with me their plans to enter college in September. It means selling their home and relocating but it's something they're both looking forward to.

The wind was still blowing when I went outside and main street was deserted as I drove through town. During the half hour drive to Carrie and Slim's, I realized how dark it was without the streetlights I was used to in the city.

Albert Heinrich

On my way to the Band office next morning, I stopped to visit Ramona, one of Bobby Allison's daughters, four miles north of Keremeos. Her house was set back from the highway among tall trees by the river bank, surrounded on three sides by hay fields. I recognized Albert, her eldest son, when he answered the door. When I asked if Ramona was home Albert replied, "You've just missed Mom and Dad. They've gone to Vancouver Island. Won't be back for about a week."

When I explained my project, he invited me in and asked if he could help. He told me what it had been like growing up in Keremeos being part white. Ramona's husband Bob is white. Albert said in high school most of his friends were white, that even as an adult he doesn't feel comfortable with some of the Native people in the valley. His family moved to the coast near Vancouver when he was a child, returning to Keremeos when he was in grade seven. He has never felt fully accepted by the Indians in the valley. He said that growing up with a white father of German descent had had an influence on the kids in his family. His parents had only recently remarried, after being divorced for ten years.

I asked for his views on the education of Native kids in the area. "This valley is not as political as some Indian bands. Bobby (Albert's grandfather) and Barney have always really encouraged kids to get an education and bring it back to the valley. They were good role models, although more passive. You knew they expected you to do things. But they never really pressed you. I remember Grandma, Bobby's wife Mary, pushing us to succeed more for material success." He described his grandfather as being more easy going. "His philosophy was, `Oh, it'll get done.' The Allisons did experience material success. They don't remember any hardship during the Depression.

"In our family, Mom pushed us all equally, boys and girls. It was important to her that we get an education. Maybe because she was the first Indian in the valley to marry white and lose her status. It was important for her to prove she hadn't made a mistake. She also lost her rights in the Catholic Church (because Dad had been married before.) She couldn't take communion when her kids took theirs. This was a double blow to her. Grandpa always knew God was a lot bigger than the Catholic Church."

Marcy Trotter

Albert's youngest sister Marcy arrived about then and joined in our conversation. I had never met Marcy before and I tried not to stare. She is short like her mother and looks like an Italian doll. Both Marcy and Albert said people had mistaken them for Italian when they were in university. She has a B.A. in Recreation Administration from the University of Alberta and is currently the Counsellor/Tutor for the Native students in the Keremeos school district. Albert has a B.A. in Physical Education and a degree in Theology.

Albert asked Marcy if she'd ever felt uncomfortable being part white. She said, "No," she had never noticed any prejudice. She was in grade five when they moved back to the valley. Marcy seemed very comfortable with who she was, very determined and straight forward.

Albert said he had his first experience with real prejudice when confronted by the principal of the Bible College he had attended. He said the man's comments took him by surprise. Both Albert and Marcy married white people from Cawston. Marcy's husband was raised on a local ranch.

Marcy and Albert agreed that a variety of things had influenced the integration of Indians and whites in the valley. Examples they suggested were ranchers helping each other. Marcy remembers "…as a kid being taken from ranch to ranch while the branding was going on," people playing sports together (her grandfather Bobby coached a men's hardball league).

Albert remembered, "Bobby and Mary were always careful how they appeared to the larger community, their dress, etc. They were conscious of the `drunken Indian' perception."

Marcy thinks it's important for Native kids not to feel singled out at school. She is careful when tutoring to go around to all students, while being sure to check on the Native kids. "They are uncomfortable with special Native days at school. They feel it singles them out, so they would rather have it after hours."

She commented, "Girls have strong role models. Boys don't." She believes that is, "Definitely a major thing," regarding success rates of students. When asked about life in the Keremeos area, she replied, "Lack of prejudice in the valley makes it hard for people to leave."

When questioned about teachers in the valley, Albert recalled Al McKee, boys' physical education teacher at the high school. "He expects 100% out of everyone. He's a really good teacher. He had a big influence on me. Mr. Drossos, too. He was a premier teacher. He would spend the time with you. `No one fails my class.'" Albert hit a responsive chord when he said that. I've never forgotten my debt to Mr. Drossos for helping me survive Algebra, or for being one of my staunchest supporters when I returned to complete my high school education. Marcy spoke highly of Campbell Dirksen, the principal of Cawston School. He had been in the district over twenty years. "He's really committed to Native curriculum. He's been a big help to Debbie and I in our jobs."

Robert, their younger brother, arrived as I was leaving. Albert described him as "the cowboy" and said he had always fitted in.

Theresa Sam

After I left Albert and Marcy, I drove south to Keremeos, noting again the shale slides on the mountains. I especially enjoyed seeing the landmark K Mountain overlooking the town, named for the giant K clearly etched in its surface by shale slides.

At the Band office I asked Theresa Sam, one of the secretaries, if she would share her views with me. Her perspective was unique because, although she has lived in the valley for ten years and has become part of a local family, she was raised in Fort

St. James. It is a small northern community in British Columbia with a large Native Indian population.

Theresa suggested we go into the office nearest the front desk. She spoke very positively about local parents. "Parents in this area get really involved in their children's education, compared to up north. If parents support kids, the kids do well in school. If parents don't support kids, the kids don't do well in school."

Theresa feels it's good for children to go back to their cultural roots. "They do better if they know where they came from, who they are. It builds self-esteem, and helps the kids do better in school. The Keremeos school district has cultural weeks. That makes nonNatives more aware of local Native culture. Even the Princeton school district brought their kids to our pow-wow grounds.

"Some districts put Indian kids in alternate programs and the kids don't get their academics. That needs to be changed. Some schools treat kids well until they get the money for them (approximately $4,000 per student in October every year from the government), then they don't care whether they stay or not."

Theresa found a difference in the teachers here compared to what she had been used to. "It's a small community. Teachers try their best with the kids. They really make an effort. Kids who are angry need a lot of counselling, preferably from a Native counsellor." She explained, "These are usually kids who move in from other areas. Up north more of the parents still drink than in this area. Then the kids think it's alright for them to drink.

"Up north a lot of boys drop out to learn trapping etc. when they're about sixteen. This is still happening to some extent." Theresa stresses to her boy the education he needs, even though he's in grade two.

Lyle, her husband, has recently taken adult education courses to complete grade twelve. He now plans to take Drug and Alcohol Training at the En'Owkin Centre in Penticton, thirty miles northeast of Keremeos. He then wants to enter the field of Social Work.

Last year Theresa took a university preparation course at Okanagan College in Penticton. She wants to study law. It would be possible for her to complete a Bachelor of Arts in three years in Penticton.

Theresa and I had just finished talking when it was announced that the office was closing for lunch.

Leon Louis

When I returned to the Band office after lunch my nephew Leon Louis was sitting outside on the bench. His hair, trimmed short across his forehead, was long in the back. I was especially interested to hear his views on education in the valley. Although he is a member of the Lower Similkameen Band, he was raised a short distance across the American border at Palmer Lake, Washington and graduated from Tonasket High School.

Leon was very serious as he talked. "The kids are doing well in school. It's after school things seem to fall apart. Things seem to come to a stop after that.

Especially the guys. Maybe it's peer pressure. They work when the (Band) office gives them a job. Otherwise they don't.

"The only ones who keep the ambition going are the ladies. The Band probably pays out a million dollars a year hiring plumbers, electricians, carpenters, etc. Our own students should be trained to do these jobs on our reserves and others nearby. Then we'd be keeping the money in our own little (Native) community a little longer.

"Our own people aren't encouraged to apply for jobs in the Super Valu, drugstore, etc. Instead they expect the Band office to provide them with a job. Then their work habits are often slack because they copy what some of the older workers do, coming in late, skipping a day, etc." He stopped to clarify, "This is only some of the students are this way. Others are good workers. It's important for the kids to start their work habits right because we have a lot of good people here. The Band could work to help the kids get jobs in the outside community. Recently, more people are trying to start their own businesses, farms, a butcher shop.

"I started working in the States for the nonNative community. I had to accept responsibility and carry a job out."

Leon would like to see the language and the culture brought into the kids' education. "The kids need to know why they are proud, what their past is, what the future is." He is very traditional. "A pow-wow is just for show. It's nothing like a sundance or a medicine dance. It's so wonderful. I wish more people could experience them." For three years Leon travelled throughout Canada and the United States studying traditional Native medicines and religions.

"Tee Pee Tot Day Care Centre is trying to teach the kids the Similkameen language. That's good. I think they also need to teach them their history. We need to teach our kids the history of other Native groups and how they had an influence on us, for example, the Sioux and Apache. We need to teach the nonNative kids what Natives are, also that we are spiritual; we are not savages. We do have a culture and traditions. To not feel sorry for us, to not feel we have our hand out begging. And, if we do, to understand why."

Leon thinks culture and traditions need to be taught in the schools. "We also need to keep up the academic education of the Native kids because times are changing. We have to keep up. Our way of life is also important, so we need to keep that up. Right now the Indians have lost their identity. They don't know what it's like to be an Indian. We need to teach the kids to respect Mother Earth and how to use her to survive. To keep giving them what is being started in Tee Pee Tots is a good idea. They need to be taught the language. The parents need to be taught too, so the kids can speak the language at home."

Leon was invited to the Oka Reserve near Montreal, Quebec, to help teach the people how to build and use sweathouses. He made four trips to Oka in a year. He was there the summer of the lengthy stand-off between the Native people and the Quebec police force.

Leon and I talked long after the office closed for the day. Eventually he left and I went to the restaurant across the street to get some supper. Before eating, I phoned Barbara, Ramona's older sister. When I had talked to her that morning she said to call her after work. She invited me to come and talk to her and her husband Henry at 7:00 that evening.

Barbara and Henry Allison

Barbara and Henry live in a new log house next to the highway on the large property where Ramona lives, near the landmark called "Standing Rock." The huge upright stone is the focus of a local Indian legend.

When I knocked someone called, "Come in." I entered a large combined kitchen-dining-living area. Barb and Henry were sitting in the living room entertaining a small boy and girl and Barb was holding a tiny baby. I was standing in the living room before they realized I had come in. When I said, "Hello," Barb looked up.

"Oh, hi, Lila. I didn't hear you."

Henry motioned me to a chair. I was introduced to their grandchildren. The young couple I had seen in the kitchen area was introduced as their son Henry Jr. and his wife Bernadette. It was explained that they live in Vernon, 100 miles northeast of Keremeos. Henry Jr. had been laid off, so had brought his family for a visit two weeks earlier. It was obvious that Barbara and Henry were enjoying their grandchildren. I marvelled, as I have for years, that Barb and Henry are the only couple I know who never age.

At times throughout the evening Henry Jr. and Bernedette joined in the conversation. They offered interesting comparisons between Indian/white relationships in Keremeos and in Vernon, where Bernedette grew up on a large reserve a few miles outside of town.

When I asked Barbara for her thoughts on why Keremeos produced so many graduates, she mentioned Campbell Dirksen, principal of Cawston Primary School. "He's a really good principal. He was in Hedley twenty years ago. He's been in Cawston twelve to fifteen years. All the teachers in Cawston started about the same time. They're all excellent with the kids. Some Hedley parents bus their kids to Cawston because of the staff. This principal and the teachers have influenced kids that are graduating" (because of the length of time they have taught in the district).

Barb continued, "The teachers have a lot of activities at the schools for parents. This builds a positive attitude toward education."

Henry pointed out, "There are lots of extracurricular activities, bussing kids to basketball, volleyball, music festivals, ancient rock paintings, skiing, pow-wows, etc. They do a lot of fund raising (parents, kids and teachers). Trips are planned a year ahead. Kids help with the planning." Henry is a school bus driver for the school district.

Barbara explained that their daughter, Tammy, enjoys pow-wows. Barb sees them as something positive for the kids to do. "Lots of kids go to pow-wows. It's a safe activity. No drugs or alcohol are allowed." She believes pow-wows have helped the boys. "No one can go who's been drinking. It helps the kids feel good about themselves. They feel comfortable being around other Indians." White people are also welcomed at pow-wows.

When asked for their perceptions about differing expectations for girls and boys, they commented, "Perhaps one reason girls may have been pushed more than boys to get an education is that they could lose their status. Boys would never lose their status. Parents may have pushed girls to be prepared in case they married off-reserve or outside the valley. (Until 1985 women lost their Indian status if they married a nonNative or a nonstatus Indian - an Indian with no status according to government). This happened to Barbara when she married Henry, who is nonstatus. The family has recently been granted status because government regulations have changed. Women who lost their status before 1985 have since been able to apply to the government to have their status reinstated and to obtain status for their children.

Barb and Henry have encouraged their kids to marry Indians so their grandchildren will have status.)

When asked about residential schools, Barbara commented that she had noticed kids who came back from residential school when she was a child were shy and withdrawn around white people and Indians. Henry said his mother who is a Sto:lo Indian from Hope, spent eight years at the Mission Residential School. She couldn't even go home for holidays. She left the school when she was eighteen. He said this really affected the way she treated her children. She became a heavy drinker.

The early settlers intermarried with the Indians. They worked right along with them and had fairly decent relationships with them. Henry's grandmother and Barbara's great grandmother married white men. Their grandmothers were very industrious, both had their own pack trains. "Indian ranchers were as successful as white ranchers. In those days they helped one another." A friend of Barbara's from the Penticton Reserve told her after a recent visit to Keremeos, "There's no lines in

Keremeos between Indians and whites." He noticed a remarkable difference between Keremeos and Penticton, although they are only thirty miles apart.

Henry Jr. thinks that Indians in the Similkameen mix more often with the white population than most Indians do, because Keremeos is in the middle of the valley. Indians have to drive through town to get to the other part of the reserve. The Indians always lived on farms and ranches and didn't cluster together. This made it easier to mix with whites who lived on neighboring farms and ranches.

Barb and Henry believe that respect between the two groups and the amount of integration between them has helped encourage Indian kids to do well in school. The kids feel accepted as part of the larger community in the Keremeos area.

Traditionally women are the power behind the men. Women who marry in from other reserves seem more aggressive. They speak out and seem to be taking the men's role. Barb and Henry feel the younger women should be less aggressive, should get behind the men and encourage them to take the lead.

This would encourage male role models and encourage men to become leaders in the community.

In Keremeos Henry Jr. felt discrimination from other Indian kids in school because he was nonstatus. He didn't feel discrimination from white kids, therefore he had many white friends.

His wife Bernedette was raised on a reserve with 1200 members twenty miles outside of Vernon. She explained, "Because the reserve is a half hour drive out of town the kids have to catch the school bus, so they can't participate in after school sports. Families, which tend to be large, planned sports and other activities on the reserve. This discourages integration. "Indians and whites don't mix in Vernon. They consider themselves different." Intermarriage between Indians and whites on the Vernon Reserve is almost nil now. There was quite a bit during the 1950s and 1960s.

Henry and his son both expressed that, because of being nonstatus, they feel insecure with the local Indians. They felt they were treated as if they were white. Both feel more comfortable in

Vernon - accepted as Indians there. Henry and Barb lived and worked in Vernon for three years. Tammy their youngest child, experienced prejudice when she went to school in Vernon. She even got into fights. In Keremeos she had lots of white friends at school, but not in Vernon.

Henry Jr. said the first time he really experienced prejudice was when he went to a dance at the Recreation Centre in Kelowna while he was attending college. Some football players threw him through a plate glass window. He was so surprised he didn't even get angry.

Barb said she has sat in meetings at conferences and wondered if the horror stories people tell about prejudice are really true. She thinks people are really lucky to live in this valley.

Barbara made some traditional herbal tea. As I drank it, I admired their beautiful home. Henry described how they had cut the logs on their own property and built the house themselves. The interior is bare, varnished logs, open up to the peak of the roof.

Barbara got out the photograph album and showed me pictures of the 1989 reunion of rodeo queens in Keremeos. Barbara had been the first of many Indian rodeo queens. We counted ten Native members of royalty, queens and princesses, in recent years.

It was 10:30 when I excused myself and left.

The time for my research had expired. Next morning I packed the car, said goodbye to Carrie and Slim, and drove back to Vancouver, pleased with the amount of data I had gathered.

Keremeos School District Personnel

Two months later I revisited the Similkameen Valley. As well as interviewing members of the Similkameen Band, I spent time visiting the schools and talking to teachers and administrators. I wanted to hear their perceptions of what factors contributed to the high graduation rate of Native students.

There are six hundred students in the Keremeos school district, attending three schools.

Approximately seventy-five of the students are Native Indian. There are two primary schools, located at Cawston and Hedley, and the Similkameen Elementary Secondary School at Keremeos, which enrolls 440 students in grades four through twelve.

I interviewed sixteen educators from two schools, all of them nonNative. They included four administrators, eight secondary school teachers, two of whom are retired, and six elementary school teachers. Twelve of them have taught in the district for ten or more years, several for more than fifteen years. Three have less than ten years experience in the district.

All the teachers spoke highly of Native students in the Keremeos district. They felt that school staffs were generally very supportive of all students and did not differentiate between Native and nonNative students. "Native kids are not a separate identity in the school." "There never was any prejudice amongst the teachers. It never was brought up that the kids were Indian." "I don't think we assumed they would be different. We just thought they were like everyone else."

Teachers praised the level of support that the Similkameen Indian Band consistently provides for its students. "Chief Barney Allison is a real advocate for education." "We have a very progressive Indian Band in the valley." "The strength of the Native community is the biggest reason for graduation rates."

Six staff members offered comparisons between the situation with the Similkameen Native people and situations with Native groups they have worked with in other parts of British Columbia: Cowichan, Kitimat, Seabird Island, Terrace and Penticton. One commented on Native/white relations in Prince Albert, Saskatchewan. Examples of comments made are:

"Usually counsellors in other places have lower expectations of Indian kids. That's not true here."

"At the school on the Seabird Island Indian Reserve near Chilliwack, they don't have the same academic success rate as Keremeos. The social success they are having will lead to great things in the future."

"Terrace doesn't have the same support for Native students as Keremeos does. The local support by the Indian Band makes a big difference. Kids get a lot of support."

"Penticton (with a large Native population) is just changing from a half time to a fulltime counselling position for Native students. Their counsellor is nonNative. Keremeos has had two fulltime positions for a number of years, filled by Native counsellors."

"At the secondary school in Penticton there are groups of good Native kids and groups of problem Native kids. There are no particular discipline problems with Native kids in Keremeos. Probably because Natives are part of the community."

"There is definitely a noticeable difference between Keremeos and Kitimat. In Kitimat, Indians were Indians, and whites were whites."

"In Cowichan there was an "Indian" look, of poverty, etc. There isn't an Indian look here."

"There is a significant difference in attitude toward Natives here than in the Prince Albert area of Saskatchewan. There's lots of mixed dating in Keremeos. It wouldn't have been accepted in Saskatchewan.

CHAPTER 2

FACTORS INCREASING
THE GRADUATION RATE

"If you kids make it, the Indian people will make it. This generation is the elastic."   Barney Allison

The Similkameen Indian Band in Keremeos, British Columbia graduated 93% of the students from their Band during the twenty-eight year period from 1963 through 1991. This high graduation rate continues in 2013 as confirmed by Marcus Toneato, principal of Similkameen Elementary Secondary School and assistant superintendent Jim Insley. That is a period of 50 years!

Are the factors contributing to this success transferable to other Native Indian Bands, other communities and other school districts?

Through research I identified several factors,

some of which are transferable to help other communities improve their graduation rates. The factors are: (1) integration of Native and white population (2) minimal attendance of Band members at residential school (3) educational support for students from members of the Native Band (4) educated parents/family members (5) academic support from school staff for students (6) strong role models (7) sports programs. Some of these factors are interrelated. They have all been described under the following four headings.

Integration of Native and White Population

Historical factors appear to have influenced the educational success rate of students from the Similkameen Indian Band. The Similkameen people were always relatively wealthy. This may have contributed to their strong sense of self- worth. Their wealth affected even initial contact with Europeans and has continued to have a bearing on their relationship with white people. Since the arrival of the first white people in the Similkameen Valley around 1860, the Native people have integrated with the newcomers. Women were encouraged to marry them to establish friendly relations between the two groups. Barbara Allison commented that, "The early settlers intermarried with the Indians. They worked right along with them and had fairly decent relationships." "Henry's grandmother and my great-grandmother married white men." From the beginning members of the two cultures worked cooperatively, hunting and fishing together. They set up ranches and farms adjacent to each other and the Native people adopted the newcomers' methods of ranching and farming (Ormsby, 1931; Thrupp, 1929). "Indian ranchers were as successful as white ranchers from the beginning. In those days they helped one another.

"Compared to neighboring groups, the people of the Similkameen were wealthy. This was due mainly to the trading of three rare items: eagle feathers for the war-bonnets of prairie Indians, red ochre, a popular face paint and soapstone for ceremonial pipes. These items were in demand as far away as the prairies" (Barlee, 1978).

The Similkameen Indians have been successful in maintaining economic stability. Some of the comments made by members of the Similkameen Band were, "When the white men came, they introduced horses. The Indians adapted quickly to horses and began raising them. Around Hedley there were a thousand horses, and around the border area at Chopaka there were a thousand horses." "Then came cattle. `Indian Edwards' had a herd of a thousand head of cattle. He would work for white people for small wages and a few head of cattle. He gradually built up his herd." "(The Indians) helped one another by working for one another and paying off in cattle or horses. There were thousands of cattle and horses." "There used to be twenty or thirty families owned cattle." This financial success has facilitated the equal status of the Native people among the white population and has had an influence on the acceptance of Native students in the school system. "If the people were dirt poor, they probably wouldn't be as well treated."

During the Depression the Indians helped people who had no work. Destitute Alberta farmers worked on some of the local ranches for up to ten years. They left their pro-educational attitudes as a legacy to their Indian employers. "During the Depression, a lot of white people came from the prairies and worked for the Indian ranchers just for their board. They were farmers who went broke on the prairies. They stayed for about ten years. During that time they influenced the Indian people's ideas about the importance of education."

Few of the Similkameen Indians attended residential school, therefore they were spared the negative educational experiences that Native children elsewhere endured in a white environment (Haig-Brown, 1988; Vayro, 1986; Redford, 1978; Native Studies, Government of Manitoba, 1971). Because of this many of their traditions have survived and their language has been retained by the older generations. Family relationships are stronger than they are among many of the Native groups who were subjected to long periods of attendance at residential schools. An additional benefit is that the Band has not been left with strong negative associations regarding education. "We're fortunate here. We're quite a ways from any residential schools so not many people went." "Catholic priests tried to force the kids to go to residential school but the parents wouldn't listen." "Residential school confused a lot of people regarding who they are."

Members of the Similkameen Band who did attend residential schools condemned the harsh system: "You have to be strong to have survived residential school." "They came in the fall with cattle trucks to the reserve in Merritt where I grew up. They'd round up all the kids whether they wanted to go or not and take them to residential school." "We were lonely. We didn't have enough to eat and they were so strict." "The kids were always hungry." "The food wasn't fit for human consumption." "Kids would steal frozen turnips from the cellar in the middle of the night to stop their hunger pains." "Some of the punishments besides the strap were having to stand in cold showers and doing without supper." "They were starving us in those schools." "Ninety-five percent of our generation never learned the Similkameen language because our parents were punished for speaking it when they were in residential school. Many parents hesitated to teach their children something they might later be punished for." "Dad said he wasn't going to allow his kids to go to residential school. He fought hard for all the kids to go to public school."

Native children were allowed to attend the public schools in the Similkameen Valley long before it was legal to do so. "Indians were in public school here before it was legally allowed." "Around 1900 Billy went to the white school near Cawston. He couldn't even speak any English." "The Indians donated land at Hedley for a school (in the early 1900s) so that the Indian kids could go to school there" (instead of going to residential school).

Having the main commercial centres of Keremeos, Cawston, and Hedley situated between the Upper and Lower Similkameen Reserves has encouraged interaction between the Native and white communities. "The Indians rode up and down the valley those days (a distance of 30 miles). There were no trucks to haul horses. I must have rode that trip at least fifty times." "Indians have to drive through town to get to the other part of the reserve. Because of this they mix more often with the white population than they do in some places where it's easier to avoid the whites." A further sign of integration is that the Band established the Similkameen Indian Administration Office in Keremeos rather than on the reserve. A school principal commented, "Locating the Band Office in the middle of town was a brilliant idea."

Both Native and white people insist that there has never been discrimination between the two groups in the Similkameen Valley. "Everyone was treated the same at school and on the job. Indians who came from other areas were surprised by this. I never felt any prejudice either at school or on the job." "There's no lines in Keremeos between Indians and whites." "During calving time Native and white ranchers used to go from ranch to ranch helping each other." "Lack of prejudice in the valley makes it hard for people to leave." "Being raised in Keremeos makes a difference. Maybe the first generations got along well with the white people and it's carried on. It's built into this community; carried down through the generations." "We've always been told to respect white people. We have to live with these people all our lives. We have to get along with them." "You don't notice racism in this valley." "People are really lucky to live here." "I never experienced prejudice until I left the valley."

Teachers also commented on the relationship between the two cultures: "There is no tension between the Native and nonNative community in the Keremeos area." "There's lots of mixed dating in Keremeos." "Being Native is not an issue in the school." "Everyone in the valley went to school together. There was no separateness. We shared experiences and therefore grew up with the same ideas and goals." "White parents are not reluctant to send their kids to the Tee Pee Tot Day Care Centre on the reserve." "Indians in Keremeos are accepted as a part of the population." "Natives aren't being patronized here." "There is mutual respect. None of this conqueror and conquered." "The kids were always friends. There was no difference." "Dating of white and Native kids doesn't even draw a glance because of the degree of integration." "The Native people here are just a part of the community." "We didn't think of them as different from us. They were part of our lives."

Sports have also been a unifying force in the Similkameen Valley and have influenced many Native students to remain in school. "Sports have contributed a lot to integration in the community. There are two or three ball clubs and annual rodeos." "Sports hold kids. Change their whole view of school." "When I was younger I told my parents I only wanted to go to grade ten, but I changed my mind because of sports once I was in secondary school." "Most of the rodeo queens here for years have been Indian." "White people are welcomed at Native cultural events such as pow-wows." "Community sports and school tournaments are all integrated. The only separate teams are the Native basketball teams."

Integration between Natives and the white population in the Similkameen Valley has fostered an atmosphere of acceptance and security. Members of the Similkameen Band feel accepted as equals and they in turn have accepted the white people. Native students benefit from this mutual respect because it is reflected in their acceptance at school. Chief Barney Allison summed it up, "Integration has always been good here. Integration is a key to the success rate of Native students in the valley."

Educational Support From Members of the Similkameen Indian Band

According to students in the Similkameen Indian Band and to teachers in the Keremeos school district, the Band is very concerned about the needs of its students. It makes every effort to support pre-school to post-secondary students emotionally, socially, academically, and financially. Teachers commented: "The strength of the Native community is the biggest reason for graduation rates. The Band knows its future." "Local support by the Indian Band makes a big difference. Kids get lots of support." "There's an awful lot of support from the Band Office." "We have a very progressive Indian Band. The children are well cared for."

In December and in June education dinners are sponsored by the Band to recognize students of all ages. "At the June dinner last year each kid got a T-shirt stating `I am the future of Similkameen.' " "Each child had to say `When I grow up I want to be....' " "The Education Dinner in December is a community potluck dinner. All the kids and parents come. Principals and teachers are invited. It's very positive." "This year it concentrated on post-secondary students. Money awards were given. The students spoke about what they are studying at university. It was good role modeling for younger students." "Most kids have aspirations. They are encouraged to `Go for it and get a better life.' " "Even kids from poor and troubled families are graduating; there are so many support systems." "If kids don't have lunches teachers just phone the Band Office and someone brings a lunch. This doesn't happen very often."

The Band gives students in grades 8 to 12 a ten dollar monthly allowance as an incentive and presents every high school graduate with two hundred dollars. The Band Office also works cooperatively with the two Native counsellors who have worked in the school district for several years. Both the counselling and tutoring programs are supported by the Band. "The Band pushed for the two counselling positions so the quality of the kids' education would be improved." The Band finances a program for the counsellors to take grade twelve students to visit the post-secondary institution they plan to attend after graduation.

Native parents support the education of their children in several ways. They have a Parents' Education Committee, they volunteer to help in the schools and are very supportive of the educational efforts of the teachers. "The Parents' Education Committee is starting to try to keep kids from being shuffled into Special Ed." "Parent groups, Native and nonNative, are very active in the valley. There are a lot of parent volunteers in the schools. The majority of Native parents are very aware of the importance of an education for their children." "Proper parenting is important in encouraging kids to carry on with their education." Parents tell their kids, "If you want to do ranching or work in the orchards, that's okay. Otherwise get an education." "Parents in this area get really involved in their children's education. If parents support kids, the kids do well in school. If parents don't support kids, the kids don't do well in school." "It's a small community. Teachers try their best with the kids. They really make an effort."

Native students are aware of having the support of their parents and grandparents. That support has been obvious for at least two generations: "I remember Grandma pushing us to succeed." "Parents of some kids are graduates. They have gone through the system and are encouraging their kids to go to school. Even some grandparents are graduates." "My mom really pushed me to go to school. She really wanted me to do law. Dad wanted me to go to school but to do what I wanted." "John and Delphine Terbasket and my grandmother Julia Qualtier told me that education was important." "Dad said to get an education because we had the opportunity." "In our family Mom pushed us all equally, boys and girls. It was important to her that we get an education." "We've always been `John and Delphine's daughters.' That's had a big effect on us. People expected us to keep going to school and to do well for that reason."

Adults in the Similkameen Band are good role models for the children. Since 1971, when they started a night school program on the reserve ("Two evenings a week for five months twenty people, including the chiefs of both Bands, met at the hall on the Chopaka Reserve to go to school.") a large proportion of them have returned to school to further their education. As a result of Carrie Allison wanting more education the night school program was organized. After four years at night school, Carrie went to a hairdressing school and became a hairdresser. She opened her own shop on the Upper Similkameen reserve and was the only hairdresser in the Hedley area. Two of the other women, Theresa Ann Terbasket and Hazel Squakin, became Native Court Workers. Theresa Ann and Hazel have since trained as linguists in the Okanagan language and Hazel went on to take teacher training at university. Hazel was the mother of nine children when she joined the night school class. To have time to study, she often worked on her school assignments late into the night.

Some years almost half of the adults in the Band have applied to attend some form of adult education ranging from short term vocational courses to full university programs. There are already several Band members with university degrees and others at various stages of a university program. These adults are modeling for the young people of the Band the value they place on education.

Since the arrival of European settlers in the Similkameen Valley the Native people have encouraged their children to benefit from the newcomers' system of education. The Similkameen Indian Band realizes the importance of education to the future of their people. As Barney Allison told his daughter, Nan, "If you kids make it, the Indian people will make it. This generation is the elastic."

According to statements made by Similkameen Band members and Keremeos school district personnel, brothers Barney and Bobby Allison have made a significant difference in the area of Native Indian education in the Similkameen Valley. Although the strength of the women in the Similkameen Band was emphasized by several informants, as was the lack of male role models, the data clearly indicated that Barney and Bobby have indeed been role models. By their vision and subtle guidance they directed the Band on a path that has resulted in an exceptionally high graduation rate of students. When over ninety percent of the adults in the Lower Similkameen Band were alcoholics, Bobby and Barney and their wives, Mary and Margaret, were nondrinkers. Some statements which support their influence in the Band and on the educational success of students are: "Bobby Allison said he wasn't going to allow his kids to go to residential school. He fought hard for all the kids to go to public school" (starting in the early 1940s). "In 1966 Bobby and Barney Allison convinced John Terbasket to attend Cody Institute in Nova Scotia to study a community planning course in alcoholism, community instability, etc. He was then to return and help his community. John became the first administrator for the Band when they took over from the Department of Indian Affairs in 1969. Bobby had spent some time with Native leaders from other areas and he and Barney were aware of some of the future needs of the Band." "Barney has been chief of the Lower Similkameen Band for more than twenty-seven years. He was a student in the night school class I taught on the reserve in 1971." "Barney feels that sports have contributed a lot to integration in the community. He was instrumental in starting the annual Chopaka Rodeo in the early 1970s." "Bobby coached a men's hardball league." "Bobby and Barney have always really encouraged kids to get an education and bring it back to the valley. They were good role models although more passive. You knew they expected you to do things but they never really pressed you." "Dad (Barney) said to get an education because we had the opportunity." "My parents (Barney and Margaret) were responsible for me staying in school." "Barney is a strong advocate of education. He is always present at the education dinners and at graduation as a guest speaker offering words of encouragement and inspiration." "Barney has a lot to do with success in education." "Chief Barney Allison is a positive influence for education. He is very supportive." "Bobby's daughter, Barbara, was the first secondary school graduate in Keremeos from the Similkameen Band" (in 1955).

Educational Support from Keremeos School District Personnel

School District personnel in Keremeos do not distinguish between Native and nonNative students. This is not a conscious decision, it is an unconscious reality. It has been true since Native students first started to attend local schools in the early 1900s. This lack of discrimination has been a strong factor in enabling Native students to feel comfortable in the schools and to realize their academic potential. An administrator observed, "Native students are not a separate identity in the schools." A retired teacher who had taught two generations of students in Keremeos commented, "I don't think we assumed they would be different. We just thought they were like everyone else."

Schools in the Keremeos district do not keep separate records for Native Indian students. After being told at the Band Office that they had no records on the number of Native students who had graduated from high school, I went to the school for the information. Principal Don McLaren's surprised response was, "Why would we keep separate records on one group of students? We keep all the records together." When asked to assist me in compiling such a list he had trouble differentiating between Native and nonNative students. Throughout the ninety minute session of leafing through seventeen years of transcripts he frequently sought clarification from the secretaries, "Is So-and-So Native or not?" To verify the list of names, making sure only Native students were included, I took it to the Band Office. Based on this example and several others I concluded that Keremeos school personnel definitely do not differentiate between Native and nonNative students.

Native kids receive a great deal of support from school staff members. In the words of former graduates: "Similkameen Secondary School is a small school so it's harder to fall through the cracks. You know everyone. The teachers are supportive and they give you a break. Some teachers have taught two or three generations of kids." "Al McKee, the P.E. teacher, expects one hundred percent out of everyone. He's a really good teacher. He had a big influence on me. John Drossos, too. He was a premier teacher. He would spend the time with you. `No one fails my class.' "

Teachers' comments regarding Native students included: "Usually counsellors in other places have lower expectations of Indian kids. Not true here. The counselling office supports kids through their difficulties by attending funerals with them, etc. Then they help them catch up." "In Science Native kids keep up very well." "There are no particular discipline problems with Native kids, probably because the Natives are part of the community." "I don't know where the Native kids get their social training but they are more polite, respectful and responsible than any other identifiable group of kids in the school. Therefore the staff are willing to put in extra time, give extra help." "The staff as a whole give any kid a chance to succeed. They don't look at the race of the child." "Kids are helped before they get into trouble." "Kids are tolerated here a long time after they would have been thrown out of other schools." "Don McLaren has a real devotion to the kids." "Keremeos graduates 100% of all grade twelve students." "It's a small school. There's lots of support for all the students." "Keremeos has had two fulltime Native counsellors for a number of years. They provide good support" (working as a team with the Band Office and with school staff.)

Native students and teachers agree that there

is no prejudice in the schools. "Frank found the school in Keremeos much better than those he was used to. There was no prejudice. He didn't feel he was treated any differently than anyone else." "The fact that teachers are fairly open (not prejudiced) helps a lot." "I've taught in Keremeos for sixteen years and have never noticed any prejudice on the staff." "Native students are so well integrated here." "Our Native kids aren't any different behavior-wise and academic-wise than the other kids. I've never heard teachers say Native kids are more difficult." "There never was any prejudice amongst the teachers. It never was brought up that the kids were Indian." "We just thought they were like everyone else." Mrs. Willis, retired school librarian said, "Indian kids have courtesy, `bred in the bone' dignity."

Native and white students do not discriminate against each other. "A visiting theatre group doing a presentation on racial discrimination surveyed the students. The results showed that the students don't distinguish between Native and white. The white kids don't think of the kids as being Native." "The kids don't view themselves much differently either." "There was no difference between white and Indian kids. We had lots of Indian friends and white friends at school. We dated white boys and had them for friends."

Native parents offered many positive comments on the schools in the district. "It's a small community. Teachers try their best with the kids. They really make an effort." "The Keremeos School District has cultural weeks. That makes nonNatives more aware of local Native culture." "Mary Beecroft was a very good teacher. She taught in Cawston." "John Drossos was a good teacher. My kids liked him."

"The teachers have a lot of activities at the schools for parents. This builds a positive attitude toward education." "There are lots of extracurricular activities: bussing kids to sports activities, ancient rock paintings, skiing, pow-wows, etc. Parents, kids and teachers do a lot of fund raising. Trips are planned a year ahead. Kids help with the planning."

Teachers also commented on the schools,

"John Drossos was such a good teacher. So down to earth." "There's been a Native curriculum in the schools for seventeen years, mainly in the primary grades." "Native cultural activities have been going on in the schools for about ten years." "The Native programs are for all students, not just Native Indians." "The School Board provides each school with money and bussing for Native cultural activities."

Campbell Dirksen, principal of Cawston School, and his staff received special praise from parents. "Campbell Dirksen was made an honorary member of the Lower Similkameen Band. A white feather was presented to him by Chief Barney Allison." "Campbell keeps communications open with Indians." When asked about this Mr. Dirksen replied, "Parents are always invited and accepted in the school. Hired go-betweens are not encouraged to speak for parents. If there is a problem parents are encouraged to come to the school to speak to the principal and/or teachers." "Campbell Dirksen is definitely a positive influence for Native education in the valley." "Campbell Dirksen is a really good principal. He's been in Cawston twelve to fifteen years and he was in Hedley before that. All the teachers in Cawston started about the same time. They're all excellent with the kids." "Teachers at Cawston School are often at the school working until 5:00 or 6:00." "That staff has been there so long that they have influenced kids that are graduating."

The Native school counsellors commented, "The principal of the secondary school tells the teachers to back off when we say the kids are going through a bad time." "Campbell Dirksen is really committed to Native curriculum. He's a big help to us in our jobs."

Teachers feel a responsibility to the students and their parents. Campbell Dirksen confided, "I keep track of kids when they go to secondary school. I still feel responsible because the kids become part of the community. Also because it's a small community and everyone knows everyone else." "The Native community is very strong. It has done a lot to instill self-esteem."

Regarding Native curriculum, teachers

commented: "I would like to see the Okanagan language taught in the schools in place of French for the kids that want it." "It would be educationally beneficial to start teaching cultural classes in the Similkameen schools, e. g., the Okanagan language and Social Studies based on Indian history."

Teachers and other educators in the district praise the Similkameen Indian Band members for the strong influence they have on the educational success of their students. "Chief Barney Allison is a positive influence for education. He speaks at the graduation dinner every year. It is a dinner hosted by the Native community to honor all Native students in the district. Principals and teachers are invited. Barney's very supportive of education." "Last year at the education dinner everyone in a post-secondary program got up and talked about why they had gone back to school, how difficult it was and why it is important for the kids to keep on." "Barney Allison is a real advocate for education." "We have a very progressive Indian Band in the valley. The children are well cared for. The Band is more financially able than many other

Bands. They are not transient as happens in some school districts." "The Band funds a program which enables counsellors to take Native grade twelve students to visit the place they plan to attend after graduation, e.g., university, job site, etc." "Local support by the Indian Band makes a big difference. Kids get lots of support." "There's an awful lot of support from the Band Office." "The strength of the Native community is the biggest reason for graduation rates. The Band knows its future." "Native kids who are successful have a strong sense of self." "Barney has a lot to do with success in education." "Barney Allison always came to the graduation. He always encouraged education."

The graduation of Native students has been encouraged and facilitated by the positive attitude of school personnel in Keremeos. The Keremeos school district supports Native students by treating them the same as they treat the other students in the schools, by having the same expectations they have for all other students. Although this school district graduated its first Native student in 1955 they have never made special allowances for Native students. It is taken for granted that these students will adhere to the academic standards of the school, will complete assignments on time and will perform in all subject areas to the best of their ability, like all other students. Graduation is an expectation at Similkameen Secondary School. According to the Province Newspaper, although British Columbia's graduation rate is seventy percent, "Keremeos graduates virtually all of their Grade 12 students" (Kilian, October 30, 1990, p. 29).

In spite of the positive relationship indicated between the Similkameen Indian Band and the Keremeos school district personnel, several Native adults, mainly parents, and two school staff members indicated that they were aware of situations in the schools that they considered to be less than satisfactory. Three Band members questioned the dedication of teachers: "Teaching is more of a job to teachers now than `a calling' as it used to be. Teachers used to put in more time and effort." "I worry that some kids are being pushed through the system, that the kids' skills are so low they are assigned rather than promoted to higher grades." "We realize a lot of teachers are just `teaching for the bucks,' so kids don't get that much attention." "Many boys are shuffled into Special Ed and the parents haven't complained. The Parents' Education Committee is starting to try to keep that from happening." One parent expressed the opinion that, "In this valley we are like white Indians. Not enough is being taught about Native identity and Native culture. This needs to be taught so that Natives as well as nonNatives know Native history. We're just beginning to learn and understand our Native belief systems. I don't necessarily believe in going back totally, but we need that connection with our past. As kids we weren't taught to be proud of being Indian, be proud of who we are. Even in high school I didn't know anything about my past. I didn't understand the reserve system, why we were on reserves or where the reserve lines were in the valley."

Comments by school staff members were: "Only one or two teachers in the district stand out as prejudiced. Often several kids are misbehaving, but a

Native kid is singled out as the troublemaker." "When there were prejudiced teachers, Indian students were protected from them."

The number of negative comments is small when compared to the majority of comments, which were very positive.

Sports Programs as a Means of Retaining Students in School

Sports have played a unique role in the educational success of Native Indian students from the Lower Similkameen Band. Sports have helped Native students become part of a group both in school and in the community. They have been the hook that kept some Native students attending school when they might otherwise have dropped out. Sports have helped to foster the self-esteem, commitment and determination essential to academic success. Two such vehicles in the Similkameen Valley have been school sports teams and Nan Allison's Basketball Club.

School sports teams, especially basketball teams, have been instrumental in encouraging Native kids to stay in school. A former graduate alleged, "Sports hold kids. Change their whole view of school. Indian kids in the Similkameen are good athletes. They do well in basketball, volleyball, baseball, track-and-field. They're all on teams. Even in grades five, six and seven kids are really into sports - soccer, basketball, baseball." "When I was younger I told my parents I only wanted to go to grade ten, but I changed my mind because of sports once I was in secondary school." One of the male graduates confided, "Sports helped keep me in school. I was involved in basketball, volleyball, and enjoyed track-and-field activities - long distance running, shotput, discus and high jump. In grade twelve I tied for top athlete of the school."

Al McKee, boys' physical education teacher commented, "Basketball is really strong in Keremeos. Some kids, boys more than girls, have maintained coming to school because of basketball. The athletic influence is definitely a strong factor in keeping kids in school. One grade twelve boy has had his ups and downs in other classes but has always done well in P.E. classes. That has helped to keep him on track. One boy really pushed himself in cross country and did well."

Teachers believe that sports play a part in the educational success of Native students. "Our Natives are good basketball players. They are skilful and are needed on the team, therefore they are not excluded." "Native kids are equal participants on the teams and in P.E. They are team members, accepted on the team." "The sports program is very important." "Sports probably helped to retain some of the Native kids in school."

The desire to organize sports activities for the young people of the Similkameen Band led Nan Allison to drop out of school at the age of sixteen to develop her natural leadership abilities. Because of her determination and commitment she helped to mold a group of twenty-nine girls from the Similkameen Band into a tightly knit sisterhood over a period of fourteen years from 1972 to 1986. These girls, the Similkameen Starbirds, not only played basketball, baseball and other sports together, they encouraged one another to stay in school "We pressured each other to stay in school." "We protected each other." "In our age group the girls disciplined each other," in regard to drugs, alcohol, etc, and influenced each other's dating patterns. "Girls don't consider white men as marriage partners." And they pressured the boys in their age group to conform, "We tried to pressure the boys to keep going. The six or seven boys we stayed close to graduated." "We screen the women the men bring into the valley." Nan pushed the girls to get their education. All but one of them graduated.

Nan recruited Agnes Bush, a retired physical education teacher, to coach the girls. For two winters Mrs. Bush worked with the girls every week. She taught them, "Winners never quit and quitters never win," and "We're only as strong as our weakest player." When I visited Mrs. Bush in her home she showed me a cherished Valentine card from Nan and the Starbirds. It was inscribed, "To the greatest person we know" and signed by all the girls.

Nan also managed the sports activities of eighteen boys from the Similkameen Band for five years. Nan believes that if the men in the Band had allowed her to continue coaching the boys, more than six of them would have graduated. "The boys ranged in age from eight to twelve years when I started working with them. I reluctantly gave up managing the team when some of the fathers started complaining that they didn't want their sons to have a female manager. They wanted the boys to have strong male role models." Instead the boys were left with no manager and no coach. Nan believes that if she had kept on working with them, the boys would have developed higher self-esteem, as the girls did, "The girls grew up with a strong self-image, good self-esteem." Nan believes that fewer of the boys would have developed drug and alcohol problems, "Boys of that age got heavily into drugs and alcohol," and that more of them would have gone on to higher education. The boys would have been exposed to the traditional beliefs and attitudes that Nan passed on to the girls and they would probably have become better role models for their sons. "While managing the basketball teams I did a lot of teaching of attitudes. I taught discipline, the meaning of authority, sportsmanship, sharing, etiquette, the importance of team work. I taught the kids that it was important when playing in other towns, if billeted out, to show proper manners and to be good ambassadors for their community. I emphasized the importance of never being lazy."

Twenty-eight of the twenty-nine girls graduated from secondary school. Eighteen of them have taken some form of post-secondary training. And as an indication of their love for sports, seven of them now coach teams. Nan served as a role model for them, they are now role models for others. Nan believes the things the girls learned will carry over and affect other areas of their lives. "It will affect how they raise their children. They will raise their boys and girls more equally. In the future boys should be given more responsibility and more encouragement to do well."

In times of crisis the girls have proven more resilient than the boys. The death of one of the boys in a car accident caused the boys' Basketball Club to fold. When one of the girls committed suicide, the girls' team recovered enough to play the following season.

Nan demonstrated for the girls responsibility and dedication and a belief that they were winners. She encouraged them to believe in themselves and in each other. She helped them discover strength in numbers. Through the Basketball Club Nan has had a lasting influence on the lives of some of the young adults, male and female, of the Similkameen Band. She had a vision for her friends and through her efforts that vision became a reality.

Sports, through school teams and Nan's Basketball Club, have provided a lasting legacy. In the past several decades, sports appear to have been the single strongest contributing factor to the exceptionally high graduation rate of Native students in the Keremeos area. The right climate was provided by the integration of the Native and nonNative people in the valley, by the strengths of the Similkameen Indian Band and by the dedication of the Keremeos school district personnel. However, by their own admission a large number of the graduates of the Similkameen Band were sustained throughout their school years by their love for sports.

Conclusions

From my study I conclude that there are several factors that have made a difference in the graduation rate of Native Indian students from the Similkameen Indian Band. These are (1) integration of Native and white population (2) minimal attendance of family members at residential schools (3) educational support from members of the Similkameen Indian Band (4) educated parents and family members (5) academic support from Keremeos school district personnel (6) good role models for students (7) sports programs as a means of retaining students in school. These factors overlap, and although I have summarized my findings under four main headings, all the factors are covered in those four categories.

Based on the experience I have had with twenty-three Native Indian Bands over a period of more than thirty years, it is clear to me that the presence of those same factors does not exist to a sufficient degree in the other Bands to significantly effect the present graduation rate of students.

I conclude that:

1.   Integration has contributed to the graduation rate by helping Native students feel welcome and secure in their environment whether on reserve, in town, or at school. Young people have benefited from the long term mutual respect that exists between the Native and white communities. That respect is reflected in their acceptance at school and elsewhere. None of the other Bands I have worked with or know of possess the degree of integration with the white population as the Similkameen Band.

2. The Similkameen Indian Band has contributed to the graduation rate by providing a strong, stable support system for Native students. The Band members contribute social, emotional, educational and financial assistance to students from preschool through post-secondary education. This support has been gradually increasing since the 1940s and 1950s when Band members such as Bobby Allison and Barney Allison realized the importance of education to the future of the Band. Only in recent years have many of the other Native Indian Bands begun to realize and support the importance of an education for their students.

3. Keremeos School District Personnel have contributed to the graduation rate by providing a safe, trusting environment conducive to learning, effective support systems, high expectations and capable, caring teachers. This accepting environment has been apparent since students from the Similkameen Bands began regular attendance at local public schools in the 1930s and 1940s. Many school districts have only started in the past few years to develop curriculum

and programs to support Native students. In many districts Native Indians are still not treated with the same respect as other students and staff members do not consistently have the same expectations for their behavior and academic progress as they do for other students.

4. Sports have contributed to the graduation rate ever since students from the Similkameen Band began playing on secondary school teams in the early 1950s. They have contributed by building trust, self-esteem and strong friendships. They have also provided a purpose for attending school and a way of being recognized as an important and contributing member of the student body and of the larger community. Although sports activities have retained many Native students in the Similkameen Secondary School, other extra-curricular activities such as music, art and drama could possibly achieve the same results in other schools. I know of no school districts in which sports or other extracurricular programs are intentionally used for the purpose of retaining Native Indian students in school.

Recommendations to Native Indian Bands

From my own experience with other Bands and based on the conclusions stated above, I make the following recommendations to Native Indian Bands:

1. Develop a vision for the future of the Band, decide what part education will play in that future and work to make that vision a reality. Believe that one or two dedicated people can make a difference.

2. Provide social, emotional, educational and financial support for pre-school to post-secondary students. Plan events such as dinners, picnics and sports days to give students special recognition.

3. Provide a variety of engaging activities, e.g., sports, music, art, drama in school and in the community for Band members of elementary school age and older. These programs should have at least the following elements: a) positive, caring teachers b) development of self-confidence and self-worth c) belief that all students can learn and that race and gender must not determine the quality of education

d) confidence in students and high but attainable standards and goals.

4.   Become involved in the children's education, e.g., form an education committee, volunteer to help in the schools, elect a member to the School Board, develop an awareness of the quality of education the children are receiving, find avenues for improving the quality of education and make the children aware of the importance the Band places on education.

5.   Work with the local community to find ways to increase integration between the Native and nonNative population. Seek input from students as future leaders of the community.

Recommendations to School Districts

From my experience working with Native Indian students and based on the factors and conclusions stated above, I make the following recommendations to school districts:

1. Seek out people in the local Native Indian community with a vision for the future and help them see the part that education can play in making that vision a reality. Believe that change can result from the efforts of one or two dedicated people.

2. Treat Native students with the same respect as other students and have the same expectations for their behavior and academic progress. Accept responsibility for the academic growth of Native students.

3. Help Native students develop self-confidence and a good self-concept.

4. Provide a variety of engaging extracurricular activities, e.g., sports, music, art, and/or drama for students of elementary school age

and older. These programs should be characterized by at least the following elements: a) positive, caring teachers b) development of self-confidence and self-worth c) belief that all students can learn and that race and gender must not determine the quality of education d) confidence in students and high but attainable standards and goals.

5. Encourage Native Indian adults to become involved in the education of children from the Band by scheduling frequent functions that involve the children, e.g., sports events, musical plays, Native cultural activities. Ensure that Native people feel welcome in the school.

6. Increase integration between the Native and nonNative communities through school activities such as concerts, Science Fairs, and sports events.

7. Hire Native Indian personnel in the schools, e.g., teachers and counsellors who provide good role models for students and who will work well with other school staff and the Native community.

8. Open the lines of communication between

Native homes and school, e.g., Home School Coordinator, counsellors, telephone calls, frequent brief newsletters.

Recommendations for Further Research

Based on the factors that emerged in this study it is recommended that:

1. A study be made of other Native Indian Bands that are successfully graduating students, to discover what contributes to their success.

2. Further research be conducted to discover the role played by sports and other extracurricular activities in retaining students in school to find how these activities can be used to increase the educational success of Native students.

CHAPTER 3

MORE SUCCESS STORIES IN NATIVE EDUCATION

"We need to start speaking with a rhetoric of success"   Don Fiddler

This chapter is based on research I conducted in 2012. I included as many examples as I could find of successful Native Indian education projects in Canada and in the United states.

Canada

Current research reveals that there are now a number of success stories in Native Indian education in Canada. More students are graduating from high school, with a better education and with a more positive attitude regarding where that education can take them. For that reason more Native young people are entering trade schools, colleges and universities. And more of them are completing their post-secondary programs. More studies are attempting to identify characteristics within individuals, Bands and schools that may encourage high school completion. More research is beginning to focus on the positive aspects of Native Indian education, seeking to determine the reasons students remain in school until they graduate.

In 2004, a very positive contribution to the growing list of success stories in Native Indian education was made by Dr. David Bell and six other researchers. They completed a study named *Sharing Our Success: Ten Case Studies in Aboriginal Schooling,* which focused on ten successful educational situations in western and northern Canada. Bell stated, "Each school in the study provided unique evidence of tangible progress being created for its students....We hope that the findings of this report may prove helpful to Canadian educators and policy makers in making changes or developing new practices that positively impact the education of Aboriginal students." The perspectives presented are those of the Native people involved and the local school district personnel. It was undertaken by the Society for the Advancement of Excellence in Education (SAEE). Three schools were selected in British Columbia, two schools in each of Alberta, Saskatchewan and Manitoba and one school in the Yukon. School populations ranged from 35% to 100% Aboriginal, and the studies included students from pre-kindergarten to grade 12. Some schools were in urban locations, others were on isolated reserves.

The report focused on the factors that contributed to the successes in the ten schools. These factors were summarized by Dr. Jo-Ann Archibald, Faculty of Education, University of British Columbia, in the Foreword of the study, "...effective leadership, creating a welcoming school climate with high expectations, caring and dedicated school staff, adequate funding and strategic use of resources, engagement with community and forms of governance, and quality programs." David Bell and his team also looked at resources that were needed to further improve the quality of education in these schools (Bell et al., 2004).

In 2007 a similar study of ten more schools was completed for SAEE by Dr. George Fulford and a team of researchers. They researched schools in central, eastern and northern Canada. The study was entitled *Sharing Our Success: More Case Studies in Aboriginal Schooling: Band-Operated Schools: A Companion Report.* It focused on four band-operated schools in Ontario, Quebec, Nova Scotia and Newfoundland, as well as six schools under provincial/territorial control: two each in Ontario and Quebec, one each in Manitoba and the Northwest Territories. There were 75 to 877 students per school, a total of 3300 students in all. The schools in the latter study had many positive characteristics in common with the ten schools in the original study that helped to account for the success of all twenty schools. Studying the success factors of these schools is helping to provide a framework for moving forward on a positive path in Native Indian education across the Canadian provinces.

In Ottawa "...one of the most important and unexpected priorities of the Harper government" is said to be a First Nations Education Act (Ibbitson, 2012). The Tories are considering a report presented in December 2011 by the standing senate committee on Aboriginal Peoples chaired by Senator Gerry St. Germain. The report is titled *Reforming First Nations Education: From Crisis to Hope.* It calls for "...the development of a First Nations Education Act for on-reserve elementary and secondary education" (Gyapong, 2011). The report recommends an education system with three levels of support for schools on reserve: schools supported by school boards which would be supported by a ministry of education. The ministry would "...set (and maintain) standards, train teachers and ensure accountability." According to St. Germain, a Metis born and raised in Manitoba, the aim is for the government to "...work in partnership with First Nations in a way that takes into consideration their culture, their language and the various aspects of their lifestyles." The system would allow each school board to modify the curriculum to meet the needs of its people (Gyapong, 2011; McGregor, 2012).

Support for a First Nations Education Act is coming from the Tories, the Senate Liberals, National Chief Shawn Atleo from the Assembly of First Nations, and Governor General David Johnston. This proposed new education system could positively affect the lives of the "...600,000 First Nations children (who) will be old enough to join the workforce in 2026" (Gyapong, 2011).

The Senate has proposed building on the Mi'kmaq Education Act in effect in Nova Scotia since 1998. It provides 3 main benefits to participating Bands: better quality education; more control of education; Mi'kmaw language, culture and history included in the curriculum of First Nation and public schools in Nova Scotia. Another benefit is stabilized funding for five year periods. Under this Act graduation rates for Mi'kmaq students have increased from 50% to a high of 70%. Mi'kmaw speakers amongst children increased from 4% to 87% between 2000 and 2004 under the Mi'kmaw Immersion Program (Impact Assessment for Participating Mi'kmaw Communities, 2004). The Act gave the Mi'kmaq people control over education for more than 2800 students kindergarten through grade 12 and management of post-secondary programs (Government of Canada, 2011).

Former Prime Minister Paul Martin has undertaken to help improve the quality of Native Indian education in Canada, kindergarten through post-secondary. He and his family have created the Martin Aboriginal Education Initiative (MAEI) to fund projects and he is involving the oil and gas industry, banks, other businesses and philanthropists to help with funding.

One of the projects Martin has sponsored is a

business course "...based on a New York project that cut dropout rates in half." This grade 11 and 12 course is now in 10 Canadian schools and is being expanded to other schools with high aboriginal enrolments. MAEI has teamed with Nelson Education to produce a textbook for this Aboriginal Youth Entrepreneurship Program. The book is geared specifically to Native youth to give them the message that "...business is a subject that applies to them" (Perkins, Globe and Mail, 2011). Martin said, "...if you can show that you can really make a difference, I think you can get the Canadian (government) onside" (Stolte, Edmonton Journal, 2012). He charges that the "...funding gaps between native and non-native schools (are) human rights violations" and is calling on the federal government to right this wrong (Buell, Metro Halifax, 2012). He states that "... there are now a number of aboriginal educators who are first rate" and could make an important difference in aboriginal schools if adequate funding was available (Stolte, 2012).

In B.C. the Ministry of Education, local school boards and local aboriginal communities have undertaken to design Aboriginal Education Enhancement Agreements in each school district that meet the specific needs of aboriginal students in the district. The overall goal is to improve academic success of aboriginal students in kindergarten through grade 12, to improve graduation rates, to integrate aboriginal culture and history into the curriculum at all grade levels for Native and nonNative students and to encourage aboriginal parents and communities to become involved at the school level. Fifty-three of the 60 school districts have signed enhancement agreements. School districts are reporting an increase in graduation levels since they developed an Aboriginal Education Enhancement Agreement.

In 2012 the British Columbia Ministry of Education appointed its first Superintendent of Aboriginal Achievement. They chose DeDe DeRose who, as a First Nations educator, has for the past 30 years filled a variety of educational posts throughout the province: teacher, principal, member of a Ministry steering committee regarding Aboriginal teachers, member of BC College of Teachers and co-chair of the First Nations Education Council, which oversees the Native Indian Teachers Education Program (NITEP) at the University of B.C. DeRose has made it a priority in her career to ensure that "…in-service workshops about Aboriginal education (were) provided for teachers in order to sensitize them to the importance of understanding historical, social, political and economic issues facing students and their families" (Young, Raven's Eye, 2005).

In her new position she will be working with the First Nations Education Steering Committee (FNESC), "…as well as with school districts and education stakeholders in B.C. to identify needs and priorities for Aboriginal education" (Hyslop, The Tyee, 2012).

In 2011-12 the graduation rate for aboriginal students was 56% according to the B.C. Education Ministry. This is up from 53% in 2010-11 and 50% in 2009-10. This is an improvement of almost 14 per cent since 2002. (The graduation rate of all B.C.

students is approximately 80%). Remarkable improvement in aboriginal graduation rates has been shown in some districts, e.g., 18% increase in one year in the Comox Valley and 36% over five years in Boundary school district.

According to DeDe DeRose, "Aboriginal education enhancement agreements, aboriginal curriculum, bringing elders into classrooms – these are some of the ways we are helping to make aboriginal students feel welcome and valued in our schools." The B.C. government is currently changing the kindergarten to grade 12 curriculum to include more aboriginal content (Steffenhagen, Vancouver Sun, 2013).

An area in British Columbia that is benefitting from the Aboriginal Education Enhancement Agreement is Sooke, which has become a leader in Aboriginal education in the province. It is a small town in School District 62 on southern Vancouver Island. In 2012 Sooke graduated 104 Native Indian students, more than double the number of graduates in 2011. In 2007 they only graduated thirty-eight percent of Native students. Now the graduation rate is almost on a par with the other students in the district (73% compared to 76%). In British Columbia the graduation rate for Native students is about 50%. Sooke has the fourth highest graduation rate of Native students in the province.

Kathleen King-Hunt, district principal for Aboriginal education in Sooke, is very positive about the progress being made. She explains that the enhancement agreement brings Native culture into the classrooms where it is integrated with other subjects. Another element contributing to increased success in the district are Aboriginal education rooms staffed with Native teachers and support workers. These rooms give students their own space, coupled with support for academic subjects, cultural activities and personal problems (Sooke News Mirror, 2012).

At the Chief Atahm School near Chase, B.C. the children are being successfully immersed in their traditional language and culture. The school is located on the Adams Lake reserve 270 miles northeast of Vancouver. It has been in operation for 20 years. In kindergarten to grade 3 all teaching is in the local Secwepemctsin language. Grades 4 through 7 are taught half in their Native language and half in English. The curriculum has been developed by teachers and parents. Elders are relied on for help in teaching the language. Traditional skills are used to teach science and other subjects, e.g., skinning a deer, smoking fish, collecting medicinal plants, singing traditional songs.

As well as developing inner strength and a sense of who they are, students leave Chief Atahm School with good academic skills. Principal Robert Matthew says, "We think that if we offer a quality education here (our graduates) will be prepared to go anywhere. And history has proven it's true. Our students here are well prepared for the public school, and many have gone to university or colleges" (Hyslop, Teacher Magazine, 2011).

Another school having success is the

community school in Bella Bella, B.C. It is in a small Native village located on Campbell Island off the mid-coast of British Columbia. In 2011 Bella Bella graduated 26 students. This is a big change from when teacher Brenda Humchitt arrived there thirty years ago and found that no high school classes were offered in the village. The school is one of the largest Native schools in B.C. with 200 students and it has a retention rate of 98%, which is higher than non-aboriginal schools in B.C. Students are "...immersed in the Heiltsuk culture." Courses such as Biology 12 and Physics 12 are offered through long distance learning in the learning support room. In place of English 12 the school offers First Nations Grade 12 English, based on Native Indian history and stories. It is recognized by B.C. universities as equivalent to English 12. Bella Bella students often score higher than the B.C. average on provincial exams (Hunter, Globe and Mail, 2011).

Vancouver, B.C. graduated 146 Aboriginal students in 2012. Each year the Vancouver School

Board (VSB) has a ceremony to honor its Native graduates. They emphasize that each graduate is a success story. There are 2200 Native students in the Vancouver public school system, kindergarten through grade 12. Although VSB is not yet satisfied with the graduation rate, Don Fiddler, Vancouver School Board's district principal for Aboriginal education, emphasized the positive."…we need to start speaking with a rhetoric of success rather than just deficit because a lot of good things are happening among our students who stay in school. There are a lot of kids who are doing well." He believes that, "Families are the greatest determinant of success in school. That is the group that protects and socializes the student to be successful."

Vancouver has been taking steps for several years to bolster the success of Native students. In 1987 they began developing a special program in elementary Inner City schools to give extra academic help to Native students in grades 4, 5, 6 and 7 in hopes that success in elementary school would carry over to increased graduation rates in high school. In

2004 VSB introduced the Aboriginal Gifts project which gives Native students fifty dollars a week scholarship money from the federal government's Urban Aboriginal Strategy, and private donors, as an incentive for passing the difficult Math 12 course. Since then more students have been successful in completing the course (Ward, Vancouver Sun, 2012).

Following numerous other initiatives, in 2010 VSB increased the number of Aboriginal staff and support workers through the Aboriginal Education Enhancement Agreement. "The agreement is a recognition that more has to be done," said Fiddler.

Merritt, B.C., 180 miles east of Vancouver, began early to put supports in place to help Native Indian students experience success in the public school system. Native students started entering the public schools in Merritt in the early 1960s. Previously, many of them had attended residential schools in Kamloops or Lytton. Before the end of the 1960s, the Merritt School Board employed a Native Home School Co-ordinator whose role was to improve communications between the area's six

Indian reserves and district schools. Robert Sterling, from the Lower Nicola Band, was the first person to hold this position and he was largely responsible for developing the role. This early intervention in Native education has paid off by the good relationships that now exist between the schools, students, parents and Indian Bands. It has also contributed to the educational progress of Native students and to the strong success in graduation rates. The number of Native students graduating from Merritt Secondary School (MSS), the only high school in the Merritt area, has tripled in recent years. It is now on par with the graduation rate of all other students in the school.

Students, parents and school staff report high levels of satisfaction with achievement in the local schools. Parents "...feel welcome in the school (MSS) and have a sense of ownership in being allowed direct access to the First Nations support workers, counsellors, or teachers. They remark on the accessibility of the teachers....

"Teachers and administrators are clear about two things: that Merritt Secondary School has high expectations, and academic expectations are the same for all students." The principal emphasized this by saying, ' Expectations are the same for everybody, and we have high expectations." One teacher said, "I don't think there are any teachers here whose expectations are different for the First Nations kids. Mine aren't, they are the same for everybody, and our expectations in this school are quite high. I expect my First Nations students will do what I ask of all of them to do" (Bell et al., 2004).

In Alberta north of Edmonton, the Wood Buffalo Region around Fort McMurray has had a good record of graduating Native Indian students for many years. It has been said that it is the most successful in graduating aboriginal students in the province. In 1998 the 1st Annual Traditional Celebration of Achievement was held in Fort McMurray for aboriginal students. There were 27 graduates. In 2002 there were 45 graduates. The numbers keep increasing. The students graduate from four high schools in the district: Father Patrick Mercredi, Westwood, Fort McMurray Composite and Chipewyan Prairie Dene. Students come from the communities of Anzac, Fort McMurray, Janvier, Chard, Fort McKay and Fort Chipewyan.

Irene Loutit, one of the organizers of the graduation event said, "The parents also need a pat on the back for their children graduating; when there are support systems at home the students are likely to succeed. I find that principals and the superintendents in the high schools here are very supportive to the Aboriginal students and this is what we need." At the end of the annual event, the local chiefs "....address the students on the importance of education....The ceremony keeps getting bigger and bigger. I find that more and more people want to come and celebrate with the graduates each year" (Gladue, Alberta Sweetgrass, 2002).

Kim Jenkins, superintendent of the Fort McMurray Catholic Board of Education, said provincial achievement testing results are high for Grade 3, 6 and 9 First Nations, Metis and Inuit

(FNMI) students. "Our students are doing significantly better than (other students in) the province, sometimes 15 to 20 per cent," Jenkins said, "Our focus has been (that) we celebrate the aboriginal culture…(Our programs are) all designed to welcome kids into the school, to improve attendance and then, when we have them, then our focus is on academics…Our result is that the aboriginal students do just as well as the other students." Jenkins credits the district's five Native liaison workers for assuring good school attendance by students. According to him, "…attendance is the key factor in student success." The school board also has a high percentage of students that continue on to post-secondary education (Cutler, Fort McMurray Today, 2012).

Centre High School for First Nations, Metis and Inuit students in Edmonton, Alberta graduated sixty-five students in 2012 who continued on to post-secondary programs. The year before 26 students had continued on to higher education. The school offers flexible schedules, continuous enrolment and a team of support staff to help students with academic subjects and with personal problems. Rick Stanley, assistant principal, said the school "…caters to students who need extra time in high school to upgrade or take extra courses for post-secondary or career requirements." The school has "…one of the highest success rates for First Nations students…anywhere in the province in terms of them going to post-secondary," Stanley said. This year it equals about 40% of the graduates (Cutler, 2012).

Naim Cardinal, an aboriginal liaison on staff at Centre High, talked about a leadership group at the school designed to give students the opportunity to be role models. "I think schools are starting to recognize that having role models for aboriginals is very important" (Sands, Edmonton Journal, 2012).

Thomas Erasmus, 1985 winner of the Tom Longboat Award as the Canadian Native Athlete of the Year, and member of the Goodfish Lake First Nation in Lac La Biche, Alberta, is a longtime advocate for Native education. Both his parents managed to evade being sent to Native residential school. "Because they didn't bear the scars of that experience, they could be a support to all our family." He said his parents really pushed him to succeed.

In 2003 Erasmus was a member of a commission that "...created a long list of recommendations of ways for the province to improve the quality of education for aboriginal students across Alberta." Three years later he was discouraged by the slow progress being made by the Alberta government toward fulfilling the recommendations. Erasmus put together an impressive group of Native and white leaders. "Their high-powered coalition held a press conference to demand the province do more to improve aboriginal education--starting with appointing an aboriginal advisory committee to work directly with the education minister and deputy minister" (Edmonton Journal, 2006). Changes in Alberta's graduation rates are now becoming visible. The four high schools in the Fort McMurray area and Centre High School in Edmonton are examples of positive change. "Alberta

Education Minister Thomas Lukaszuk and Advanced Education and Technology Minister Greg Weadick have said the government wants to see more aboriginal students graduate and move into post-secondary programs (Sands, 2012).

Dawson City, Yukon has made impressive strides in developing First Nations education programs and increasing graduation rates. Until 1985 the graduation rate of native students from high school was very low. In 2010, 88% of the First Nations students in grade 12 graduated. Joann Vriend, who has taught in Dawson City for twenty-five years, summarized how these improvements in First Nations education and graduation rates were accomplished.

"I went to Dawson City to teach in 1985. I asked the principal at the time what the rates of graduation were for native students. He said there may have been some native graduates in the past, but he couldn't recall any. A lot of native kids were in alternative programs that led nowhere. However, many First Nations parents wanted improvement and a dialogue began. The settlement of land claims in the 90s made a difference. The Tr'ondek First Nation invested in businesses and provided jobs for its members. As more people had regular employment, family life improved, and parents wanted more for their children. This included wanting their children to graduate from high school.

"When I first went to Dawson I was the Learning Assistant (LA) for K – 12. Eventually an LA for the elementary was hired and I worked in the high school for many years. I did a study in the late 90s, for the superintendent at the time, to track what percentage of students were graduating, what percentage of First Nations students were graduating, and whether they were continuing on to seek further education. The study revealed that the graduation rates for First Nations students at that time were approximately 2% lower than for other students in Dawson City."

Over a period of time, the Tr'ondek community, teachers and school board worked together to develop programs that helped to improve the educational experience and graduation rate of First Nations students.

"One thing we noticed at the school was that it was more common for First Nations students to neglect their homework, especially as they got into the upper grades. We speculated that First Nations parents seemed to feel it was up to the students to get their work done. Accepting this as a cultural difference, we encouraged these students to take one less course, which still allowed them to graduate. It gave them a free period in which to do their homework, and there was a teacher there to help them with it. We had a policy whereby, if a student failed a course with 45% or better, we gave them the opportunity to do an extensive assignment for that course, in order to make up the percentage points to pass the course. The Tr'ondek First Nation opened a youth centre—students could go there just to spend time, there was homework help after school, and activities in the evening. The Tr'ondek First Nation had an education committee, and they put pressure on the school to help in getting students to graduate.

Staff responded. Resource room programs were strengthened to become programs that led students back to regular classes. Robert Service School used the tutoring program administered by the Learning Disabilities Association and funded by the Department of Education. Any time a student appeared to be falling behind, this after school service was offered to the family and to the student. There was also a Homework Club funded in the same way. The school has tried, over the years, to keep every student in school—tracking down students who are not attending and working with their families to try to get them to engage in their own education.

"Sports are definitely a big part of keeping teenagers in school, and Dawson is no exception. Volleyball, hockey, soccer and baseball are all popular. The Tr'ondek First Nation started what they call "First Hunt" a number of years ago—they take students out on the land for three or four days, teach them hunting skills, kill a moose or caribou, teach them how to dress it out, put on a feast in the community, show slides of the trip."

Joann Vriend sums up her conclusions of improvements in graduation rates of First Nation students: "I think that settlement of land claims, the resulting creation of jobs, and emphasis on graduation have made a big difference in Dawson."

Other provinces in Canada have developed initiatives to improve the quality of aboriginal education. In Ontario in 2007 the McGinty government started an Aboriginal Education Strategy aimed at increasing the success of Native Indian students in kindergarten through grade 12. The curriculum includes Native culture, history and traditions to be taught to all students (Ontario Government, 2009).

United States

Several of the north central American states are working together to improve American Indian education. Minnesota, Iowa, Nebraska, North Dakota and South Dakota are introducing programs to teach both American Indian and nonIndian students about American Indian history and culture. Following the research of Dr. William Demmert (2001) they are including Native language instruction for Native students because "...research shows a direct link between language instruction and improved Indian student achievement." Dr. Demmert's research "...has been the foundational work for improving achievement of Native American students across the nation" (McCallum, Minnesota Public Radio, 2007). He is an Alaskan Native and a former federal education official. Demmert's research has shown that Native American students needs can be met and their achievement improved by requiring teachers to have a good grasp of local American Indian history and culture and by the inclusion of Native history, culture and language in the curriculum. He also emphasizes that home, community and school need to be jointly involved in a student's education.

In 2007 South Dakota passed an Indian Education Act that requires "...Indian culture and history to be incorporated into state academic standards." Twelve percent of students in the state are American Indian (McCallum, 2007). South Dakota is also using some of the guidelines from Montana's successful "Indian Education for All" K - 12 program. In four years in Montana the program led to improved achievement of Native American elementary students. Reading scores in grades 3 through 5 increased by 25% and math scores improved 11% (Elementary Native American Task Force, 2010).

Minnesota, another state working to improve the education of American Indian students, is "...considered a leader in Native education....(It) requires beginning teachers to have a working knowledge of tribal history and culture, and provides scholarships to train American Indian teachers" (McCallum, 2007).

In 2010 Nebo School District, south of Salt Lake City in Utah, graduated 94% of their American Indian students. For the past ten years they have a graduation rate over 88%. This is up from 37% thirteen years ago when they started the Title VII American Indian program. The program was developed by Eileen Quintana of the Nebo School District, who is now the coordinator. It is "...exclusively for American Indian students, cultivates a pride and knowledge of culture through art projects and powwows while integrating a math, science and literacy curriculum." Quintana feels the program works because it is supported by parents, the school district and the staff. Throughout the school year Quintana and her staff oversee the approximately 300 American Indian students in the district, meeting with them regularly to provide help with homework and projects. They also hold regular workshops with parents. "We try to listen very carefully to what parents are telling us." Camp Eagle is a summer component to the program which enables students to take part in activities that are oriented to their culture and traditions. Quintana says"...the success of Nebo's program is due to the way teachers adapt their style to engage students" in a curriculum that is culturally relevant.

Shirlee Silversmith, director of the Utah Division of Indian Affairs, is very supportive of the Title VII American Indian program in Nebo. She suggested that one thing other school districts could do "...would be to make the curriculum more multicultural, incorporating history and traditions into classrooms that teach math and science" (Wood, The Deseret News, 2012).

Oregon, Washington, Montana and Idaho took part in a study involving 306 American Indian high school graduates. The study analyzed the role of schools in helping students succeed. Students reported that teachers had the strongest influence on their educational success. They appreciated caring teachers who treated students with respect and who were generous with their praise (Coburn and Nelson,1989).

At their high school graduation ceremony in Hayward, Wisconsin, twenty-one Native American students were honored by their parents, school staff and tribe, the Lac Courte Oreilles (LCO) tribe in 2012. They were each presented with an eagle feather in recognition of their accomplishment. Gordon Thayer, chairman of the Tribal Governing Board was the keynote speaker. He told the graduates, "We have a history of being leaders in education. You are future leaders. The strength of our tribe is our people. Never accept mediocrity. Rise above that and be whatever you want to be. Strength is measured in difficult times." Thayer commended the family members of the graduates for a job well done (Sawyer County Record, 2012).

Dr. Majel Boxer, a Native American, graduated

in 2008 from the University of California at Berkeley. She is a professor at Fort Lewis College in Durango, Colorado. When asked what advice she would give Native American students, she said, "My advice would be to welcome any type of educational opportunity....I went to a number of summer camps - even for science - when I was a young girl....Say yes to anything, especially educational. It's important for Native peoples to pursue education....to go into all fields of study so that we increase our presence in our own home communities, but also in the outside world (Moya-Smith, Indian Country Today, 2012).

Fort Lewis College where Dr. Boxer teaches is one of only two American colleges that guarantees a waiver of tuition fees to all American Indian students. This guarantee is part of a sacred trust that was created in 1911 between the tribes and the federal government. At that time Colorado was given a land grant of more than 6000 acres by the federal government that was the previous site of an Indian residential school. In return Colorado promised to maintain an educational institution at that location and to waive tuition fees for American Indian students. [The other tuition free college for American Indian students is Minnesota Morris.] (Cowan, Durango Herald, 2012).

In 2010 General Colin Powell and his wife Alma wrote an open letter to the American people. It was included as a Foreword in Building a Grad Nation (Balfanz et al., 2010). The letter focused on improving graduation rates for minorities, including Native American students. In part, the Powells stated, "We must do more to understand what factors have enabled some communities to experience break through improvements and apply what is working to communities that are still languishing." In the report some of the topics researched to support success in education for students were: "enhancing adult supports inside and outside the classroom, parent engagement, researching and investing in innovation to support student success, researching what works, and disseminating the best practices " (Balfanz et al., 2010).

In Arizona Professor Willard Gilbert, a member of the Hopi tribe, and a multicultural professor at Northern Arizona University - Flagstaff, is working to improve the Native American graduation rate. "The way to provide Native students an avenue to succeed," according to Gilbert, "is to incorporate Native language into the curriculum along with Native oral history, legends and greater involvement of Native elders in the classroom." He believes this will provide an avenue for increasing students' interest in the STEM program, which emphasizes science, technology, engineering and math. In working to develop educational standards, Gilbert is partnering with Harvard University and the National Indian Education Association "…to draft and disseminate Native cultural standards throughout Indian country and develop teacher assessments." Willard Gilbert is past president of the National Indian Education Association and a member of the Campaign for High School Equity (CHSE). CHSE "…focuses on high school education reform and aims to eliminate achievement gaps for Native students (Roller, Yuma Sun, 2009).

In Winterhaven, New Mexico, the Quechan Native people are making education a priority. "Native American history goes hand in hand with American history," Mike Jackson Sr., Quechan tribal president said. "As a tribal government, we're working with San Pasqual (high school) to make sure Quechan students are not left out, and working with Schoneman (district superintendent) to bring better quality education to Quechan students." Native American students make up 54 percent of the 180 students at the San Pasqual Valley Unified High School District in Winterhaven.

David Schoneman agreed with Jackson, "We've got a good relationship with the Quechan Tribal Education Center. Our district has a family feeling and it helps motivate students to succeed. San Pasqual has intervention programs in place that help motivate at-risk students to graduate. They also have Native teachers who work in after school programs at elementary and high school levels, teaching Native cultural programs. "We're fortunate to have that relationship with the tribal community. We couldn't do it alone," Schoneman said. "What would help even more is to have Native graduates return to San Pasqual as teachers because when the kids see that, they learn there's an open door to the professions" (Roller, Yuma Sun, 2009).

This chapter included examples of programs and practices in Native Indian education that have been successful for the people that have used them. I encourage others to search out more stories of success, to draw on them and on the programs included here. Expand on them, combine them and change them to create programs that will inspire more young people to remain in high school, to graduate and to engage in post-secondary pursuits that will enrich their lives and the lives of their people.

CHAPTER 4

RELATED LITERATURE

A review of the related literature concerning Native Indian education was undertaken to ascertain the factors influencing educational success. An effort was made to find studies relating to educational successes of Native Indian Bands in Canada and the United States. Historical events were reviewed to discover their relationship to educational success.

Although there have been numerous studies in Canada and the United States on Native Indian education, the majority of them focus on the problems preventing students' continuation in school, the lack of success of Native Indian students and the high dropout rate (More, 1984; Burnaby, 1982; King, 1978; Goucher, 1967; Mulvihill, 1960; Mendelson, 2008; Balfanz et al., 2010). Other studies describe the variety of Indian education projects and programs offered by school districts and other educational organizations (More, 1989; Canadian Education Association, 1984). Few, however, focus on educational successes of Native Indian students. One study that contains information on students from the Similkameen Band combined data gathered from several Okanagan and Thompson Indian Bands, making it impossible to isolate information relating only to the Similkameen students. In the literature reviewed for his study Dr. More did not find one school or program that reported long term success. He states that, "Although long term successful situations exist, they are seldom evaluated" (More, 1984, p. 29).

Part of the literature reviewed detailed the concerns of educators, politicians and Native Indian leaders regarding the lack of educational success of students and the need to find ways to encourage them to graduate from high school.

The literature reviewed here is under the headings: Before Contact With Europeans, Early Postcontact, and A Brief History of Native Indian Education.

History of the Similkameen Indians

Before Contact With Europeans

According to written historical accounts about the central interior Native people of British Columbia, excavated burial items indicate that, compared to neighboring groups, the people of the Similkameen were wealthy. This was due mainly to the trading of three rare items: eagle feathers for the war-bonnets of prairie Indians, red ochre, a popular face paint, and soapstone for ceremonial pipes. These items were in demand as far away as the prairies (Barlee, 1978).

Teit gives detailed descriptions of life among the Upper and Lower Thompson Indians around the end of the nineteenth century (Teit, 1909; Teit, 1898). The country of the Thompson people borders on the valley inhabited by the Similkameen Indians. Much of Teit's information can be applied to the Similkameen because the two groups had many things in common. Further background information related to the Similkameen Indians is provided in

Interior Salish (British Columbia Heritage Series, 1971), although they are not mentioned by name. Because of this, the information must be treated as general to the area; specifics cannot necessarily be applied to the Similkameen people. The book gives general background including food gathering, implements, religion, family life, community life and intergroup relations. A description of the history of the Upper and Lower Similkameen people during the late 1800s and early 1900s provides further background information (Hudson, 1980).

Early Postcontact in the Similkameen Valley

When horses were introduced to the area the Similkameen Indians began to build up large herds of wild horses. These were gradually replaced by herds of cattle when the Native people followed the lead of white ranchers and began to set up cattle ranches (Thrupp, 1929; Ormsby, 1931). In some cases, ranches were later divided up into farms (Mitchell et al., 1980), although many of the ranches exist today as part of the Lower Similkameen Reserve. By this time the nomadic way of life was being curbed by the number of white settlers taking up land. The demand for land led to the establishment of Indian reserves (similar to reservations in the United States), starting in 1860 (May et al., 1986; New Brunswick Human Rights Commission, 1973).

A Brief History of Native Indian Education

In 1920 attendance at residential schools became compulsory for Canadian Indian students 7 to 15 years old. In the United States this had happened in 1870. Until that time parents had a choice as to whether they sent their children to the residential schools and for how long (Redford, 1978; Native Studies Government of Manitoba, 1971). Before residential school attendance became compulsory, day schools for elementary school children operated on many reserves. Because only about half of the children enrolled in day schools attended on a regular basis, the Canadian government decided that this method of education was less than satisfactory. Residential schools were chosen as an alternative.

From 1870 to 1928 in the United States, and from 1920 until 1960 in Canada, the majority of Native Indian students were isolated from the rest of society by being educated in residential schools financed by the government and operated by various religious denominations. It was believed that this would lead to the assimilation of Native people into the white society. A detailed account of life in the Kamloops Indian Residential School at Kamloops, B.C., based on interviews with former students, shows the negative effect of one such school on the lives of members of the Native Indian bands from the central interior of British Columbia (Haig-Brown, 1988; Vayro, 1986).

Finally the governments realized that residential schools were not accomplishing the planned assimilation, nor were they being particularly successful at educating Native students. Few students achieved higher than a grade 5 education (Hawthorn et al., 1960). It was decided that a better approach might be to integrate Native students into public schools. School districts signed agreements with the federal government to provide education for Native Indian students (Stahl, Journal of American Indian Education, 1979; Canadian Education Association, 1984). Most American Indian students were attending public school by 1934, after the passage of the Johnson-O'Malley Act (Stahl, 1979). In Canada enrollment of Native students in public schools increased rapidly after 1960: 11,000 students in 1961, 25,000 in 1964 and 33,000 by 1968 (fifty-three percent of all Indian children of school age) (New Brunswick Human Rights Commission, 1973).

Another significant change for Native people in Canada occurred in 1960 when they were finally granted the right to vote in government elections. However, it was not until the policy paper "Indian Control of Indian Education" was prepared in 1972 by the National Indian Brotherhood and adopted by the Canadian government in 1973, that Native people were finally given some power to control Native Indian education (Indian Control of Indian Education,

1980). The result was that by 1984 there were 187 Band operated schools on reserves throughout Canada, and 450 of the 575 Bands were administering all or part of their programs (Canadian Education Association, 1984). In spite of the changes that have occurred in Native Indian education since 1960, and the increase in numbers of students attending high school, the number of Native students completing grade 12 in Canada and in the United States is still only about 50%.

A third major change that occurred for Canadian Native people in the 1960s was the return of adults to school to continue their education. The trend started in 1962 when a large proportion of Native Indians enrolled in high school courses for adults. In the United States, this move of Native adults to continue their education happened about the same time. In British Columbia between 1970 and 1977, 9113 Native Indian adults enrolled in upgrading classes, fifty-seven percent completed their courses (Blunt, 1978). Approximately thirty percent of the adult population took upgrading courses during this period (Blunt and Thornton, 1978). In January 1971 twenty members of the Upper and Lower Similkameen Indian Bands started an upgrading class on the Lower Similkameen Reserve. Classes continued on this reserve for several years, until all Band members wishing to attain a higher level of education had done so.

By the late 1970s, as adults completed high school education, many of them began attending universities and other post-secondary institutions. Enrollment by Native Indians in vocational schools and universities began to gradually increase. In 1949 only 58 Canadian Indians were attending post-secondary education (Anderson and Nieme, 1969). By 1969, 235 Native people were enrolled in university (New Brunswick Human Rights Commission,1973). This was only one-tenth of one percent of the Native population. Between 1960 and 1970 there were 233 Native graduates from university. Participation of Native Indian students in post-secondary education grew considerably between 1969 and 1980. By 1981 the average number graduating per year was 250 (Canadian Education Association, 1984).

As the number of students continued to increase, so did the cost of post-secondary education. In 1969-70, 808 students participated in post-secondary education at a cost to the Canadian government of $436,408; in 1980-81, 4792 students participated at a cost exceeding $18 million. The budget for 1982 was more than $28 million. Costs for post-secondary education continued to rise until the government decided to put a ceiling on the funding, and to encourage Native Indian Bands to take over the responsibility for deciding how their allotted funds would be used to finance students from their Band seeking post-secondary education.

Native Indian Bands are now expressing concern about the shortage of educational funding (Bell et al., 2004; Mendelson, 2008). Since they are not being provided with adequate funds, they are having to make choices as to which types of training they will fund and which students qualify for the funding. Shortage of funding by the federal government is one of the major stumbling blocks for Native Indian students seeking a post-secondary education. Native Bands, governments, school districts and families are focused on increasing the number of Native Indian high school graduates. As they succeed in accomplishing this goal, it will lead to increased frustration of Native youth, their families and their Bands if funding is not made available by the federal government to provide them with post-secondary training. The next goal for those seeking increased graduation rates is to convince the federal government to adequately fund post-secondary education for Native Indian students.

RESOURCES

Original Resources

Anderson, D., & Niemi, J. A. (1969). *Adult education and the disadvantaged adult*. Syracuse, NY: Eric Clearinghouse on Adult Education.

Barlee, N. L. (1978). *Similkameen: The pictograph country*. Summerland, BC: N. L. Barlee.

Blunt, A., & Thornton, J. E. (1974). *Participation in an Indian adult education program*. Vancouver, BC: Adult Education Research Centre, University of British Columbia.

Blunt, A. (1978). *Educational levels of adult status Indians in British Columbia*. Vancouver, BC: University of British Columbia.

Blunt, A., & McKinnon, D. P. (1978). Indian adult education in British Columbia. *The Journal of Education*, *18*. Vancouver, BC: Faculty of Education, University of British Columbia.

Bogdan, R. C., & Biklen, S. K. (1982). *Qualitative research for education*. New York: Allyn and Bacon.

British Columbia Heritage Series: Our Native
   Peoples, Vol. 3. (1971). *Interior Salish.*
   Victoria, BC: Department of Education.

Burnaby, Barbara. (1982). *Language in education
   among Canadian Native peoples.* Toronto, ON:
   OISE Press (Ontario Institute for Studies in
   Education).

Canadian Education Association (1984). *Recent
   developments in Native education.* Toronto,
   ON: Canadian Education Association (CEA).

Coburn, J., & Nelson, S. (1989). *Teachers do make a
   difference: What Indian graduates say about
   their school experience.* Portland, OR: Research
   and Development Program for Indian
   Education, Northwest Regional Educational
   Laboratory.

Department of Indian Affairs (1982). *Indian
   education paper: Phase 1.* Ottawa, ON:
   Education and Social Development Branch,
   Canadian Government.

Goucher, A. C. (1967). *The dropout problem among
   Indian and Metis students.* Calgary, AB: Dome

Petroleum Limited.

Haig-Brown, C. (1988). *Resistance and renewal: Surviving the Indian residential school.* Vancouver, BC: Tillacum Library.

Hawthorn, H. B., Belshaw, C. S., & Jamieson, S. N. (1960). *The Indians of British Columbia: A study of contemporary social adjustment.* Toronto, ON: University of Toronto Press and University of British Columbia.

Hudson, D.R. (1980). *The Okanagan Indian curriculum project.* Penticton, BC: The Okanagan Indian Curriculum Project.

Indian control of Indian education: Practical applications. (1980). Winnipeg, MB: National Indian Brotherhood Conference.

Kilian, C. (1990). *No uproar over missing kids.* Vancouver, BC: Province Newspaper, Pacific Press, 29.

King, A. R. (1978). *Native Indians and schooling in British Columbia.* Victoria, BC: University of Victoria.

Lincoln, Y., & Guba, E. (1985). *Naturalistic inquiry.*

Beverly Hills, CA: Sage.

Mitchell, D., & Duffy, D. (1980). *Bright sunshine and a brand new country: Recollections of the Okanagan Valley 1890-1914*. Victoria, BC: Queen's Printer for British Columbia.

More, A. J. (1984). *Okanagan Nicola Indian quality of education study*. Vancouver, BC: University of British Columbia.

More, A. J. et al. (1989). *Indian education projects and programs in B. C. schools*. Victoria, BC: Ministry of Education.

Mulvihill, J. P. (1960). *The dilemma for our Indian people*. Ottawa, ON: National Library.

Nairne, D. (1985). *Community profile of the Similkameen Native community: 1985*. Vancouver, BC: David Nairne and Associates Ltd.

Native studies Amerind history supplement 9-12. (1971). Winnipeg, MB: Department of Education, Province of Manitoba.

New Brunswick Human Rights Commission (1973). *Human rights and the Canadian Indian: A continuing program of education in human rights*. Fredericton, NB: New Brunswick Department of Labour.

Ormsby, M. A. (1931). *A study of the Okanagan Valley of British Columbia*. Vancouver, BC: University of British Columbia. Unpublished M. A. Thesis.

Redford, J. W. (1978). *Attendance at Indian residential schools in British Columbia, 1890-1920*. Vancouver, BC: University of British Columbia. Unpublished M. A. Thesis.

Spradley, J. P. (1979). *The ethnographic interview*. New York: Holt, Rinehart and Winston.

Spradley, J. P. (1980). *Participant observation*. New York: Holt, Rinehart and Winston.

Teit, J. A. (1898). *Traditions of the Thompson River Indians of British Columbia*. Boston and New York: Memoirs of the American Folk-lore Society, Vol. VI.

Teit, J. A. (1909). *Publications of the Jessup North Pacific Expedition: The Thompson Indians of B. C.*, *1*(4). New York: American Museum of

Natural History.

Thrupp, S. L. (1929). *A history of the Cranbrook district in east Kootenay.* Vancouver, BC: University of British Columbia. Unpublished M. A. Thesis.

Vayro, C. H. (1986). *Invasion and resistance: Native perspectives of the Kamloops Indian Residential School.* Vancouver, BC: University of British Columbia. Unpublished M. A. Thesis.

Williams, D. (1988). *Naturalistic inquiry methods.* Provo, UT: Brigham Young University. Unpublished manuscript.

Updated Resources

Alberta pressed to improve aboriginal education. (2006). Edmonton: The Edmonton Journal.

Aman, C., & Ungerleider. (2008). Aboriginal students and K - 12 school change in British Columbia. *Horizons, 10*(1), 31-33.

Balfanz, R. et al. (2010). *Building a grad nation: progress and challenge in ending the high school dropout epidemic*. Baltimore, MD: Johns Hopkins University.

Bell, D., Anderson, K., Fortin, T., Ottman, J., Rose, S., Simard, L., & Spencer, K. (2004). *Sharing our success: Ten case studies in Aboriginal schooling*. H. Raham (Ed.). Kelowna, BC: Society for the Advancement of Excellence in Education (SAEE).

Boettcher, T. (2012, June 1) Hayward high school native american graduates honored. *Sawyer County Record*. Retrieved from http://www.haywardwi.com/

Buell, S. (2012, July 12). Former PM Paul Martin calling for aboriginal education reform. *Metro Halifax*. Retrieved from http://metronews.ca/news/halifax/

Burdett Kilroy, L. (1991). *An ethnographic inquiry into reasons for the secondary school graduation rate of the British Columbia Similkameen Indian Band*. Provo, UT: Brigham

Young University. Unpublished Doctoral Dissertation.

Cowan, E. (2012, July 6). A historic promise: Fort Lewis college tuition waiver still changing lives for better. *Durango Herald*. Retrieved from http://indiancountrytodaymedianetwork.com/

Cutler, L. (2009, January 30). Catholic school board proud of economic performance. *Fort McMurray Today*. Retrieved from http://www.fortmcmurraytoday.com/

Elementary Native American connection task force report: executive summary. (2010). Sioux Falls: South Dakota Indian Education.

Fulford, G., Raham, H., Stevenson, B., & Wade, T. (2007). *Sharing our success: more case studies in Aboriginal schooling: Band-operated schools: A companion report*. Kelowna, BC: Society for the Advancement of Excellence in Education (SAEE).

Gladue, Y. I. (2002). Record number of Aboriginal students graduate. *Alberta Sweetgrass*, *9*(6), 11. Retrieved from http://ww.ammsa.com/node/25786

Gyapong, D. (2011, December 26). Senate report calls for urgent First Nation education reforms. Canadian Catholic News. Retrieved from http://www.wcr.ab.ca/

Hunter, J. (2011, April 12). B.C. native school a world apart; a much better world. *The Globe and Mail*. Retrieved from http://www.theglobeandmail.com/

Hyslop, K. (2011, September 6). How Chief Atahm elementary became a success story. *The Tyee*. Retrieved from http://thetyee.ca/

Hyslop, K. (2012, June 11). Province's first superintendent of aboriginal achievement appointed. *The Tyee*. Retrieved from http://thetyee.ca/

Ibbitson, J. (2012, January 8). Tories fashion native education system to improve life on reserves. *The Globe and Mail*. Retrieved from http://www.theglobeandmail.com/

Largest aboriginal grad class ever in SD 62. (2012, May 16). *Sooke News Mirror*. Retrieved from http://www.sookenewsmirror.com/

Logie, P.R. (1990). *Chronicles of pride: a journey of discovery*. Calgary, AB: Detselig Enterprises Limited.

Logie, P.R., Burdett Kilroy, L., & Overgaard, V. (1991). *Chronicles of pride: a teacher resource guide*. Calgary, AB: Detselig Enterprises Limited.

McCallum, L. (2007, May 16). *States told to improve American Indian student achievement* [Radio broadcast]. Minneapolis, MN: Minnesota Public Radio. Retrieved from http://www.mprnews.org/

McGregor, J. (2012, January 23). First nations gathering to grapple with education gap. *CBC News*. Retrieved from http://www.cbc.ca/news/

Mendelson, M. (2008). *Improving education on reserves: a first nations education authority act*. Ottawa, ON: Caledon Institute of Social Policy.

Moya-Smith, S. (2012, July 7). Award-winning native scholar says education is important. *Durango Herald*. Retrieved from http://indiancountrytodaymedianetwork.com/

Ontario Ministry of Education, (2009). *Aboriginal education in Ontario*. Retrieved from http://www.edu.gov.on.ca/eng/aboriginal/supporting.html

Mi'kmaq Education Act: Order adding the Paq'tnkek Band to the schedule to the Mi'kmaq education act. (2011). *Canada Gazette Part II*, *145*(21). Retrieved from http://www.gazette.gc.ca/gazette/home-accueil-eng.php

Perkins, T. (2011, September 12). New high school textbook aimed at aboriginal youth means business. *The Globe and Mail*. Retrieved from http://www.theglobeandmail.com/

Roller, W. (2009, January 13). Group aims to boost Native American graduation rate. *Yuma Sun*. Retrieved from https://indiancountrytodaymedianetwork.com/

Sands, A. (2012, April 13). Aboriginal graduates aim high. *Edmonton Journal*. Retrieved from http://www2.canada.com/edmontonjournal/

Stahl, W. (1979). The U.S. and Native American education: A survey of federal legislation. *Journal of American Indian Education, 18*(3), 28-32.

St. Germain, G., & Dyck, L. E. (2011). *Reforming first nations education: from crisis to hope: report of the standing senate committee on aboriginal peoples.* Retrieved from http://www.parl.gc.ca/

Steffenhagen, J. (2013, February 16). More native students graduating from high school, report says. *Vancouver Sun.* Retrieved from http://www.canada.com/vancouversun/

Stolte, E. (2012, June 12). *Funding issues stymie native schools: Martin. Edmonton Journal.* Retrieved from http://www2.canada.com/edmontonjournal/

Vriend, J. (2013). *Improvements in First Nations education in Dawson City, Yukon.* Unpublished Personal Notes.

Ward, D. (2012, June 9). *Young aboriginals conquer the odds. Vancouver Sun.* Retrieved from http://www.canada.com/vancouversun/

Wood, B. (2012, July 4). American Indian program successful in Nebo district. *The Deseret News*. Retrieved from http://www.ksl.com/

Young, G. (2005). Another first for education trailblazer. Raven's Eye *9*(3), 3. Retrieved from http://www.ammsa.com/publications/ravens-eye/

APPENDICES

Appendix A

Maps of Similkameen Indian Reserves

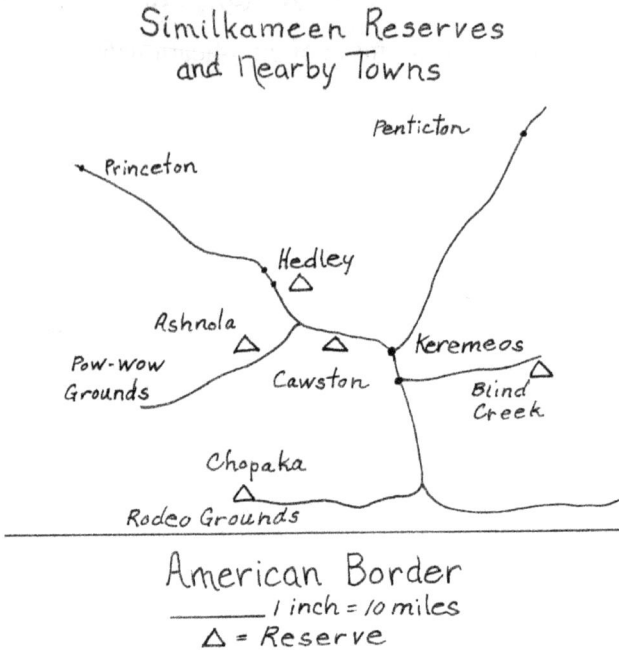

Similkameen Reserves
and Nearby Towns

Penticton

Princeton

Hedley
△

Ashnola
△   △   Keremeos
Pow-wow   △
Grounds   Cawston   Blind
Creek

Chopaka
△
Rodeo Grounds

American Border
_____ 1 inch = 10 miles
△ = Reserve

North America

▲ = Similkameen

Appendix B

Percentage of Graduates from the Similkameen Indian Band

Year	Graduates	Percentage	Dropouts
1991	7	100	0
1990	4	100	0
1989	1	50	1
1988	6	100	0
1987	4	100	0
1986	5	71	2
1985	5	83	1
1984	2	100	0
1983	4	100	0
1982	1	100	0
1981	1	100	0
1980	5	100	0
1979	1	100	0
1978	1	100	0
1977	3	100	0
1976	3	100	0
1955-75	13		
Total	**66**		**4**

About the Author

Lila Burdett grew up in the Similkameen Valley of British Columbia, Canada and is related to some of the Native Indian people of that area. She taught school for twenty-five years throughout the province, working with Native and non-Native students from elementary school through adult education. Her teaching experience caused her to recognize the unique situation in the Similkameen Valley where a high percentage of Native students graduated from high school. *Yes Indeed! It Takes a Village! A Model For Education* is the product of research Lila conducted on Native graduation rates in the Similkameen Valley for her Doctorate in Education.

Lila completed a Bachelor of Education at the University of Victoria and a Master of Education in Education Administration at the University of British Columbia. She received her Doctor of Education in Curriculum and Instruction from Brigham Young University in Utah.

www.lilaburdett.com

lilaburdett@hotmail.com